SOMME BATTLE STORIES

A BATTLE STORY

Somme Battle Stories

RECORDED BY
CAPTAIN A. J. DAWSON

ILLUSTRATED BY
CAPTAIN BRUCE BAIRNSFATHER

Published for
"THE BYSTANDER"
BY
HODDER AND STOUGHTON
LONDON   TORONTO   NEW YORK
MCMXVI

CONTENTS

CHAPTER I
"WHAT IT'S LIKE" IN THE PUSH . . . PAGE 1

CHAPTER II
THE SPIRIT OF THE BRITISH SOLDIER . . 20

CHAPTER III
THE MORAL OF THE BOCHE 34

CHAPTER IV
AN IRISH OFFICER DESCRIBES THE INDESCRIBABLE 49

CHAPTER V
CLOSE QUARTERS 61

CHAPTER VI
THE DEVIL'S WOOD 73

CHAPTER VII
THE COCKNEY FIGHTER 86

CONTENTS

CHAPTER VIII
"WE DON'T COUNT WOUNDS IN MY REGIMENT" . . 97

CHAPTER IX
A REVEREND CORPORAL 107

CHAPTER X
BROTHERS OF THE PARSONAGE 119

CHAPTER XI
THE AUSTRALIAN AS A FIGHTER . . . 132

CHAPTER XII
NEWS FOR THE O.C. COMPANY AT HOME . . 142

CHAPTER XIII
"STICKFAST" AND HIS OFFICER . . . 154

CHAPTER XIV
A COOL CANADIAN 165

CHAPTER XV
THE HOSPITAL MAIL-BAGS 177

CHAPTER XVI
THE DIFFERENCE 190

CONTENTS

CHAPTER XVII
WHAT EVERY M.O. KNOWS 200

CHAPTER XVIII
THE SOUTH AFRICAN 211

CHAPTER XIX
"IT'S A GREAT DO" 219

CHAPTER XX
ON THE WAY TO LONDON 230

CHAPTER I

"WHAT IT'S LIKE" IN THE PUSH

THERE is nothing of the professional publicist about the average wounded soldier, officer or man, now landing day by day at Southampton. They are all more concerned—thank goodness!—with action than speech; with doing things and getting them done, rather than with describing them.

It is not, of course, that these heroes of ours are either unwilling or unable to talk. They are almost invariably, and no matter what the nature of their wounds, in the highest of good spirits; delighted

2 WHAT IT'S LIKE IN THE PUSH

to pay a visit to Blighty; happy to have had the chance of playing the fine part they have played in the great Allied offensive; absolutely assured as to the victorious outcome of the Push. But they have no very accurate notions as to the relative values of the different, disjointed, staccato, frequently vivid bits of information they have to dispense. With matches, or scraps of paper, or a nicotine-stained forefinger made to serve as pencil in the nearest conveniently dusty surface, they will give you elaborate expositions of the tactics they have helped to work out. Their little lectures on the strategy of the Push are frequently couched in language more graphic, racy, and convincing than the most free and easy of Generals ever permits himself to use. And their lovable faces sometimes show a glimmer of disappointment, for that one does not take copious notes regarding these demonstrations. But, on the other hand, they deprecate with almost pitying wonder the notes one does jot down from time to time in talk with them, when (by accident) they enrich one with some vivid, stabbing little thrust of triumphant scene-painting likely to provide an answer to the constantly reiterated question as to " what it's like" in the Push.

"Oh, I say, you know, don't bother about that guff. Everyone knows about that, of course. But, if you really want to know what the plan was in the —— show, I can tell you in a minute, so far as our Brigade went. You see, zero was

——, and we were on the right flank of the ——," etc.

At the moment one has specially in mind a young Company Commander, a Captain of the ——; almost the last wounded officer to be landed from the hospital ship —— on a certain recent night. He had a good deal of the descriptive gift, and was perfectly unconscious of his occasional use of it. One strained his indulgence a good deal, and took many notes while talking with him. What one sets down here are just the bits he regarded as "guff"; convinced that "everyone knows about that, of course." His fluent strategy and tactics—but I promise they shall be preserved in the archives of his grateful country.

"Eh? Oh, just an ordinary front line

trench, you know; rather chipped about, of course, by the Boche heavies, you know; but—— Oh, hang it, you know what the ordinary fire trench looks like; along the north side of the Mametz Wood we were. What? Oh, yes, we were packed pretty close, of course, while we were waiting; only got there a little before midnight. My chaps were all in splendid heart, and keen as mustard to get the word 'Go!' I was lucky; met my friend G—— almost directly we got in. He's had months in that bit of the line, and knew every twist of it, so was able to give me tips. He took me along to his dug-out, after I'd got all my chaps in position, and gave me some jolly good hot café-au-lait.

"Tell you a funny thing about that

dug-out after. Good dug-out, with a darned sight better overhead cover than most, or it wouldn't have been there, after the pounding the line had had in the week before. G—— had a magnificent arrangement for cooking. I forget the name of the stove; but you pump it up like a bicycle tyre, and then it burns like the deuce; gives you a hot drink before you can turn round. I'm going to have one before I go back. We had two good-sized kettles, and after we'd finished our drink we ran a regular canteen for about half an hour; boiling up café-au-lait as fast as the machine would turn it out, and dishing it out all along the line of my fellows, in their mess-tins. The weather was jolly just then; but there'd been a lot of rain, and the trench was in a beastly state.

WHAT IT'S LIKE IN THE PUSH

You know what it's like, after a lot of strafing, when you get heavy rains on the churned-up ground. It was like porridge with syrup over it, and we were all absolutely plastered, hair and moustaches and everything, before we'd been half an hour in the place. The Boche was crumping us pretty heavy all the time, but it didn't really matter, because for some reason he didn't seem to have got our range just right, and nearly all his big stuff was landing in front, or behind, and giving us very little but the mud of it.

"What did worry me a bit was his machine guns. His snipers, too, seemed fairly on the spot, though how the devil they could be, with our artillery as busy as it was, I can't think. But I know

8 WHAT IT'S LIKE IN THE PUSH

several of my sentries were laid out by rifle bullets. I particularly wanted to let the others get a smoke when they could, seeing we'd be there three or four hours; helps to keep 'em steady in the waiting, you know; but we had to be mighty careful about matches, the Boche being no more than a hundred yards off. I hate the feeling of that stinking porridgey clay caking on your hands and face, don't you? But one didn't notice it, after a bit, because it was the same all over. But one had to watch out for rifles and ammunition, and that, you know. Pretty easy to get all the rifle barrels bunged up, in the dark, you know. Our Adjutant came along about three, checking up watches and giving us Divisional time. Mine was all right; never stopped once from the day I bought it till that left wrist of mine was hit. See! It registers my first hit—3.26. I'll keep that; souvenir; but I'm afraid it's done as a timekeeper.

"Just before three I got my position right in the middle of my company We were going over at 3.25, you know. The trench was deep there, with a hell of a lot of mud and water; but there was no set parapet left; just a gradual slope of muck, as though cartloads of it had been dropped from the sky by giants—spilt porridge. I wanted to be first out, if I could—good effect on the men, you know —but I couldn't trust myself in all that muck; so I'd collared a rum-case from ——'s dug-out, and was nursing the blooming thing, so that when the time came I could plant it in the mud and get a bit of a spring from that. Glad I did, too. I passed the word along at a quarter past to be ready for my whistle ; but it was all you could do to make a fellow hear by shouting in his ear. Our heavies were giving it lip then, I can tell you. I was in a devil of a stew lest some of my chaps should get over too soon. They kept wriggling up and forward in the mud. They were frightfully keen to get moving. I gathered from my sergeant their one fear was that if we couldn't soon get going our artillery would have left no strafing for us to do. Little they knew their Boche, if they thought that.

"I thought I could just make out our artillery lift, about a minute and a half before the twenty-five, but I wouldn't swear to it. On the stroke of the twenty-five I got a good jump from my rum-box, and fell head first into a little pool; whizz-bang hole, I suppose; something small. It loosened two of my front teeth pretty much. I'd my whistle in my teeth, you see. But I blew like blazes directly I got my head up. Never made a sound. Whistle full of mud. But it didn't matter a bit. They all saw me take my dive, and a lot were in front of me when I got going. But I overhauled 'em, and got in front.

"I believe we must have got nearly fifty yards without a casualty. But it's hard to say. It wasn't light, you know; just a glimmering kind of a greyness. Not easy to spot casualties. The row, of course, was deafening; and we were running like lamplighters. You remember our practice stunts at home? Short rushes, and taking cover in folds of the ground. Remember your file of direction, sir; dressin' by the right; an' all that. Oh, the boys remembered it right enough. But, good Lord, it wasn't much like Salisbury Plain. We were going hell for leather, you know. You think you're going strong, and—whoosh! You've put your face deep in porridge. Fallen in a shell-hole. You trip over some blame thing and you turn a complete somersault, and you're on again, not quite sure which end of you is up; spitting out mud, wondering where your second wind is. Lord, you haven't a notion whether you're hit or not. I felt that smack on my left wrist, along with a dozen other smacks of one sort and another, but I didn't know it was a wound for an hour or more. All you thought about was trying to keep your rifle muzzle up; and I guess the fellows behind must 've thought a bit about not stickin' us with their bayonets more'n they could help. I was shouting ——, the local name of the regiment, you know. The boys like it. But my sergeant, who was close to me, was just yelling: ' Down 'em, boys ! ' and ' Stick 'em ! Stick 'em ! ' for all he was worth.

"My lot were bound for the second line, you see. My No. 12 Platoon, with 13 of ' D,' were to look after cleaning up the Boche first line. There was no real parapet left in that Boche front line. Their trench was just a sort of gash, a ragged crack in the porridge. Where I was there was quite a bit of their wire left; but, do you know, one didn't feel it a bit. You can judge a bit from my rags what it was like. We went at it like fellows in a race charge the tape; and it didn't hurt us any more. Only thing that worried us was the porridge and the holes. Your feet sinking down make you feel you're crawling; making no headway. I wish I could have seen a bit better. It was all a muddy blur to me. But I made out a line of faces in the Boche ditch; and I know I gave a devil of a yell as we jumped for those faces. Lost my rifle there. 'Fraid I didn't stick my man, really, because my bayonet struck solid earth. I just smashed my fellow. We went down into the muck together, and another chap trod on my neck for a moment. Makes you think quick, I tell you. I pulled that chap down on top of my other Boche, and just took one good look to make sure he was a Boche; and then I gave him two rounds from my revolver, with the barrel in his face. I think I killed the under one too; but can't be sure.

"Next thing I knew we were scrambling on to the second line. It was in the wire of the second line that I got my knockout; this shoulder, and some splinters in my head. Yes, bomb. I was out of business then; but as the light grew I could see my chaps having the time of their lives inside that second line. One of 'em hauled me in after a bit, and I got a drink of beer in a big Boche dug-out, down two separate flights of steps. My hat! that beer was good, though it was German. But look here, I'm in No. 5

train, that that chap's calling. I must get ashore. Just want to tell you about that dug-out of G——'s in our own line, you know. It was four o'clock in the afternoon, and we'd got the Bazentin Wood all right, then, when my orderly, who never got a scratch, was helping me back, making for our dressing station. We crawled into what had been a trench, and while I was taking a breather I sort of looked round, and made out a bit here and a bend there. Begad, it was the trench we started from!

"Seems nothing, but you've no idea how odd it was to me; like dropping into a bit of England, after about a century and a half in—in some special kind of hell, you know. Seemed so devilish odd that any mortal thing should be the same anywhere, after that day. Not that it was the same really. My rum-case was in splinters, sticking up out of the porridge, and I found my map-case there; torn off my belt as we got over at 3.25. 'Won't be much left of that dug-out,' I thought; and I got my orderly to help me along to see. Couldn't find the blessed thing, anyhow. Went backwards and forwards three or four times. Then I spotted the head of a long trench stick that G—— had carried pokin' out through soft earth at the back of the trench. The orderly worked that stick about a little, and the earth fell away. It was just loose, dry stuff blown off the roof of the dug-out, and blocking the little entrance. Came away at a touch, almost, and there was the little hole you got in by. I worried through, somehow. I was really curious to see. If you'll believe me, the inside of that dug-out—it looked like a drawing-room to me after—after the outside, you know—it was just exactly the same as when we'd left it the night before. There was the fine stove we made the café-au-lait on, with a half-empty box of matches balanced on the side of it, and the last empty tin of the coffee stuff we'd used, with the broken-handled spoon standing up in it, just as I'd left it; and G——'s note-book lying open, and face down on an air pillow, in his bunk—most extraordinary homely.

"There was I, looking at his note-book and his hold-all, and poor G—— dead. Yes, I'd seen his body. And the rats, too; the rats were cavorting around on the felt of the roof, happy as sand-boys They didn't know anything about the Push, I suppose. By the way, we found only dead rats in the Boche trenches. They say it was our gas. I don't know; but there were thousands of dead rats there; and millions of live fleas; very live they were. I must get. Cheero!"

CHAPTER II

THE SPIRIT OF THE BRITISH SOLDIER

THERE is no vestige of any falling off in the general level of high spirits and confidence among our wounded officers and men from the battlefields of the Somme. One writes of battlefields in the plural, because in this Push there have already been a score and more engagements which, as we used to judge war, would take rank as very notable and sanguinary battles; just as there have been, literally, many thousands of individual acts which, in war as we have known it in the past, would have won for those responsible the very highest distinctions we have to offer.

"I don't know what the dispatch writers, let alone the military historians, are going to do about this Somme fighting," said an elderly Major, wounded in hand and shoulder, on the Bapaume-Albert road, below Pozières. "I saw rather a wider sector than some other officers, simply because it happened I had to get to and fro several times between our Brigade Headquarters and three of our battalions. I assure you I could easily compile a volume of bald records of individual acts of heroism and the heroism of isolated sections, taking only what I saw with my own eyes. But I should hesitate to do it, because of the implied injustice to the troops on other sectors. I've talked with lots of officers between the trenches and here, including one Divisional Staff officer and two of Brigade Staffs from different parts of our front, and I gather the same impression from all. The things I saw would have been exceptional, very exceptional, and the sort of things that pages and pages were written about—before this war. But they weren't in the least exceptional, as incidents of this present Push go. Such things have been happening, literally, all along our line, and during every hour of every day and night since July 1st."

"Does that tally with your experience?" one asked a Company Commander who was leaning beside us on the ship's rail waiting for his time to go ashore for the train. His left arm was in a sling and bandages were swathed about his head.

"Funny! I was just asking myself that very question. I was just thinking," replied Captain ———. " I was wondering how I'd manage if somebody asked me for a dozen names from my own Company, for men to receive distinctions. I tell you it would be a devil of a job, and one I'd much rather not have. Suppose I try to think, on the other hand, of any one man in my Company, or in what I saw of the rest of the Battalion, since July 1st, whom I'd just as soon have been without, a man who didn't play the game as well as he might have done. Gad, do you know, there's not a blessed one, not a single one. And, what's more, I haven't heard of one in any other unit, not a single one, and one hears a devil of a lot, one way and another, bucking with this man and the other all the way between there and here, you know.

"'Fraid I'm not much of a praying man; but, tell you what, if I'd set to work praying on the night before we went into this show—and, mind you, I daresay lots of chaps not previously given that way did pray that night. It's a big thing, you know, taking your men into a real large scale battle for the first time, when they were all civilians a little time back, and perhaps you were the same yourself—if I had, on that last night of June, I reckon what I should have prayed would have been that my Company should accomplish just about half what it did. 'Pon my soul, I shouldn't have dared to ask that they should do all that they actually did when the time came. I should have thought that was asking a jolly sight more than was reasonable. No, I'd have asked for about half what I got, and thought myself thundering lucky if I got it. As it was, I'm perfectly certain that a company of Guardsmen, with ten years' soldiering behind each man of 'em, couldn't have done more than my chaps did. They mightn't even have done quite so much. You see, our chaps felt the honour of the New Army was at stake, and its reputation all to make. We'd told 'em what the Boche newspapers said about 'em: how Kitchener's men didn't count seriously, and all that; and, by gad, they went into the scrap like knights of the olden time with their ladies lookin' on, you know; as though the New Army would stand or fall in history according as each single one of 'em carried himself in this show. You couldn't check 'em; nothing was too bad for 'em; and, I give you my word, nothing you can possibly say will be too good for 'em."

"Well, Sergeant, what's yours?" The inquiry was addressed to a fine upstanding sergeant of the Middlesex, who elected to walk ashore instead of being carried, though he was glad of a comrade's shoulder to lean on. A year or two ago the question might have suggested an American bar, but not on the landing stage at Southampton in these days.

"Oh, I got it just below me thigh, here, sir; nothing to write home about, anyway. I ought to be back this way again in a week or two. I hope I will. You see, sir, the second sergeant in my platoon got it fairly in the neck—proper bad, I'm afraid he is. They do say he may have to lose his right foot. Anyhow, he won't be back for some time, if at all; and it's bad for the platoon for the two of us to be away. Now they've made such a fine start I want to be with 'em an' keep 'em up to it. Though you wouldn't have said they wanted much keeping up to it, sir; not if you'd seen 'em at it. I reckon they saved the Battalion's flank there between Authille an' Ovillers; an' there's no sort of doubt they smashed the flank of the Boche battalion. He'd got a reg'lar nest o' typewriters there; machine guns, I should say, sir. We stood it for a bit, an' then my officer he began to get pretty mad with 'em. Always was a bit on the hot-tempered side, you know, sir; but as good an officer as ever I served with.

"'Here, damn their German eyes!' he says, just like that, when he see our chaps a-droppin'. 'We'll get these devils in the flank,' he says. 'They're not goin' to tell off my platoon that way. Come on, Sergeant,' he says; 'at the double now. Get those bombers of ours close up here behind me.' We fairly raced then for their right flank, an' all there was of us tumbled down into their ditch all of a lump. 'Bombers here!' yells my officer. He'd got two machine gun bullets in him then. Much he cared for that. We got our bombers up, and—well, as my officer said, sir, we did fairly give 'em hell after that. The platoon went through that trench like a dose o' salts, as ye might say, sir. Worried along it, like terriers in a rat earth. Never so glad in me life to have plenty of bombs. We bombed the trench fair empty; an' any Boche that missed the bombs, well, he got the steel, an' got it good an' hard; in an' out, an' in again every time, to make sure.

"An' that's how our Battalion was able to make such a good advance, sir. The rest of our Company was layin' doggo while we promenaded down that bloomin' trench; an' when my officer gave the word—he'd got a third bullet in him, then, sir, not to mention bomb splinters an' the like o' that—they come on like a cup-tie football crowd, an' the rest of the Battalion after them. They went over that first line with hardly a casualty, barrin' just a few from shrap; an' if they didn't give the Boche what for, in his second an' third lines, I'd like to know.

"My officer was fair runnin' blood by then. He got so many splinters, you see, sir, about the head an' face, besides the three bullets he'd got in him. I found him sittin' on a Boche machine gun lightin' a fag; a cigarette, I should say, sir. The Boche machine gunner was there, too; only he'd never smoke no more cigarettes, nor fire no more machine guns. He was done up pretty nasty, sir, was that gunner. But his gun was all right, because I saw two of our own M.G. section firing of it not many minutes later.

"I found him sittin' on a Boche machine gun, lightin' a fag."

I tried to make my officer let me help him back for dressin', but he wouldn't have it—not then. He smoked his cigarette, while I put the Platoon on cleaning out dug-outs in that trench. I don't mean the mud, you know, sir. We knew we weren't goin' to hold the trench, because we was pushin' farther on. No, but a good many Boches had taken cover in them dug-outs; an' what wouldn't come out when we gave 'em their own bat, ye know, sir—' Kommen Sie hier,' an' all that—well, they had their choice between bomb an' baynit, as ye might say.

"There was a few of 'em played the game pretty well, I will say. They'd a young officer with 'em, an' they fired at us as fast as we could get near the mouth o' their dug-out. We didn't want to hurt the beggars, but we'd got our job, same's they had theirs; an' in the end theirs was bombs—in the neck. But most of the others jumped to the word, an' come out quick an' lively on the order. We got forty-seven of 'em, very little damaged. We disarmed the lot, an' when we joined up with the rest of the Company my officer took that bunch of prisoners back to our old lines by himself. Got two of the biggest to carry him at the rear of the squad on two rifles. He had his revolver in one hand and a Mills bomb in the other.

"'Cheero, Sergeant!' he says to me. 'Keep the boys a-movin' till I get back.' But bless you, sir, they don't want any telling. No more'n terriers want tellin' to get after rats. I was wounded half an hour after that; an' nex' time I saw my officer was down at the dressin' station. I only saw the one German officer—that boy in the dug-out. I think that's one reason why the Boche is losin' heart a bit, an' shows himself pretty ready to be taken prisoner. His officers do keep most uncommon well out of the way; very different from ours. An' I suppose it makes their men feel the game is up. But they fight real well till you're right on top of 'em. I'll say that. Only, man for man, when it comes to it, they can't live alongside our chaps, ye know, sir—not they."

CHAPTER III

THE MORAL OF THE BOCHE

"Yes, I think you may take it Master Boche will never again set foot on the ground we have won from him this month, and I think he knows it. But, although it's mighty hard to get, the ground we've got from him is the least of the things we've taken from the German Army, as I see it. The main gain is in the changes wrought in the two armies—the Hun's and ours—since July 1st. And that you can't reckon in figures. Begad, there aren't any figures big enough for the reckoning."

THE MORAL OF THE BOCHE

These were the words of Lieut-.Colonel ———, Commanding Officer of the ———th ——— ———, spoken just before he landed from one of the hospital ships. His wound, one is glad to say, is a slight one, affecting one hand only, and this gallant officer himself regarded with some irritability the action of the medical authorities in separating him from his unit at all at the present time.

"I asked for a dressing, and they insist on giving me a trip to Blighty. However, thank goodness, I can trust my Second-in-Command, and I shall be back with my Battalion before very many days are over."

A wounded Captain from another battalion was sitting beside us in the companionway, and nodded thoughtfully over the

Colonel's reference to those of our recent gains which cannot be measured in villages or in thousands of yards.

"Yes," said the Captain, "it's the blow to the Boche moral that counts more than the ground."

"Moral. It's one of those words that people are constantly using," said the Colonel. "I wonder if the general public have any very clear idea what it covers. They use so many words now which don't really give 'em pictures, and words that don't convey pictures to the average mind aren't very informing, you know, really. When I've been home on leave I've found all sorts of people talking glibly of dug-outs, fire-trenches, barrages, consolidation, and so on, with never a hint of a picture in their minds of what the words really stand for.

" Fighting's a pretty queer business, you know, when you come to think it out, especially this sort of tornado of fighting we get now, and for twentieth-century men, lots of whom never had so much as a shot-gun in their hands till a year ago. It's more of a miracle than people at home will ever understand, is the New Army. And one of the most miraculous things about it is that at the present moment it is carrying on fighting of a kind vastly more terrible than any that the world has ever seen before, and, mark you, carrying it on with as fine a steadiness, with as much stubbornness, and as much dash, too, as any veteran army known to history has ever shown.' And if that isn't something of a miracle—well, you ask any Commanding Officer with more than ten years' service behind him.

"This business of fighting—fighting continuously and cheerily in the presence of devastating casualties—has a good deal in common with swimming and bicycling and things of that sort in which instinct plays a big part; horse-riding, too; anything that demands perfectly smooth co-ordination of thoughts, nerves, muscles, and—well, and spirit. The material supplies are essential, and in the fighting we've got before us now any failure in the material supplies must mean complete and most bloody failure all along the line. But there are other essentials, too. Every experienced leader of soldiers knows it; aye, and prays over it, if he happens to be that sort. But I suppose nobody can describe it; define it, I should say."

(The Colonel and the Captain were clearly thinking hard, in this odd interlude in their journey from shell-swept trenches to quiet English hospitals. They nodded occasionally one to another, as two men who perfectly understood the matter in hand, and entirely agreed that it could not be explained.)

"Your Staff arrangements may be perfect, and your material all there, you know, but if the other thing is missing, or weak, wrong in any way—well, the fighting doesn't come off; that's all there is about it. You can't measure it or weigh it up, any more than you can measure a cool breeze on a sultry day, but you can feel it rippling through the ranks, just as clearly as you can feel the little breeze. And God help you if you feel the absence or the failure of it, because in fighting there can be no success without it. But we've never been without it for a moment in this Push."

(The captain nodded, slowly and emphatically, beating time, and underlining his assent with his cigarette.)

"I tell you this New Army's got it, for keeps," continued the Colonel. "If you start thinking about the balance and steering of a bicycle you're going to run into the kerb or something—if you start thinking. But if you *know*, hand and mind and nerves all one—why, she goes, like a charm. Fighting's rather like that; plus heat and anger, and din and fury, and—Fight, you know.

THE MORAL OF THE BOCHE 41

"I've been in this show since it began, since the morning of the 1st, you know. Our chaps have remained much the same all through, except for one thing. At the outset they had duty in their minds, doing their bit, you know—their job. Now they've got victory in their blood. They've got to real grips with the Boche. They've found he can fight all right. They've seen he's got to. And they've found he's splendidly equipped. But they've found something else. They've found they can beat him. They've found they're just as well supplied and backed up, and a bit better. And, above all, they've found that when it comes to actual grips, knee to knee work, they can beat the Boche every time. They've found they are better men and in better heart;

which they certainly are. That's the only change so far as they're concerned. That's the advance they've made. And I can tell you it's a mighty big one; bigger than anything you'll measure in kilometres.

"But it's not so big as the other part of the advance they've made. They've accounted for hundreds of thousands of Boches, killed, wounded and prisoners. But they've done more, far more. They've hit every single Boche soldier the German High Commands have put up against 'em, and hit him very hard, and very much where he lives. And, for aught I know, they've hit every other German, every Hun that lives, whether he's in uniform or not."

"By God, they have!" interposed the

laconic Captain, with several emphatic nods.

"Double-edged business, you see," continued the Colonel. "For every ounce of moral you gain you take at least one from the enemy."

"One pound, sir; at Mametz, anyway," said the Captain.

"Well, maybe a pound. My point's this: the Hun—poor devil!—has been very carefully taught. The Boches are regular artists at propaganda. He's been taught, ever since he scratched into the lines we've taken between Thiépval and Combles, that the very most the contemptible English could ever do would be to hold their line, to sit still, until such time as the All Highest was ready to give the word to sweep them into the sea.

Offensive movement was quite impossible for these make-believe soldiers of ours. We were all shopkeepers who did not know one end of a rifle from another, and too soft, anyhow, to stand up for a moment against real, live Huns, once the Hun had made up his mind to move. We were cruel, cowardly devils, who would torture and kill any worthy German who was misguided enough to fall into our hands; but we were not soldiers: our soldiers had all been killed by the valiant German Army in the very beginning of the war, and a real offensive was utterly impossible for us. I've talked to lots of prisoners, and I assure you that's the sort of thing they've all been taught, and that's what they believed.

"I tell you, it would have been better

for Germany to-day if her leaders had told fewer damned lies in the past; better in a thousand ways. It would have been a deal better for the Hun to-day if they'd taught their soldiers that the British Army was their most deadly and formidable enemy. They're beginning to see it now — too late. Their organisation is so complete, their subjection of their people so brutally thorough, and, mark you, their teaching of their soldiers is so good, that they'll go on fighting automatically whatever happens. And they are perfectly equipped. The material is all there, the most formidable fighting machinery in the world is there; but the indefinable something, the thing that enables you to balance and steer your bicycle so easily and naturally without thought, the spirit you want to feel rippling through your ranks like a cool breeze—if you are to win; they've lost that, and we've got it, got it for keeps.

"People who try to measure the importance of the Push by the ground gained, or even by the casualties inflicted, will fall a long way short in their estimate of what it all means. The object in war is the destruction of the enemy, and the most important asset any enemy has is his spirit—the moral of his troops. Since July 1st our New Army has inflicted a crushing blow upon the enemy's moral. With the same troops the Boche can never again achieve the same ends. With the same troops on our side we can achieve greater ends. It's partly the successful bravery and dash, and the

THE MORAL OF THE BOCHE 47

stubborn endurance of our troops, and the tremendous weight of our munitions, that have so reduced the Boche moral on the Somme, and it's partly what the Boche himself has done, in the matter of long and careful teaching based on lies. Our chaps have let in the light of a little truth into the Hun's lines. It would have done 'em no harm if they'd been fed on truth. But they've been fed on lies, and the new diet's upset their digestion. In my opinion, what's been accomplished this month would have been a big gain to the Allies if our casualties had been five times what they have been. Napoleon may have been right when he said an army marched on its stomach; but, believe me, a modern, educated twentieth-century army fights on its nerves and spirit. And that's where we are immeasurably ahead of the Boche, and a long way ahead of our position of even last June."

CHAPTER IV

AN IRISH OFFICER DESCRIBES THE INDESCRIBABLE

THE mellow Irish voice of Lieut. M—— was the first to welcome me on board one of the hospital ships on a recent fine morning. One was glad to find this very popular Platoon Commander a "walking case." From others one had already heard much of the fine and dashing work done in the present Push by the Irish Regiment to which M—— belongs. But there were certain other officers whom it was necessary to see at once on this particular steamer, and, knowing of old Lieut. M——'s nimbleness with his pen, one bade him sit down in the ship's companion-way forthwith, and write out a full, true, and particular account of the Great Push.

"Give us the realities, real pictures, something much more informing than any of your letters I have seen," he was told. Perhaps one made some other remarks not conspicuously more reasonable. Here, at all events, is what he wrote, in indelible pencil, on the thin pages of an Army Book 155, the cover of which bore the stains of French trench dust and English blood. There may be little here to indicate the dashing gallantry, the dogged, always cheery bravery of M——'s Irish fighters; but it is worth reading, all the same, and as for bravery—well, there is

DESCRIBING INDESCRIBABLE 51

not a battalion on the British front, between Thiépval and Guillemont, which has not earned imperishable honours and distinction since the 1st of July :

"What you say about my letters home may be entirely deserved, my dear Skipper; but it is also, I think, quite unavoidable, even apart from the necessary censor restrictions. Let me tell you, sir, as one not wholly devoid of practical literary experience, that what you are looking for is simply not to be had. The business of this Push—of any other important phase of the war, for that matter— is too big for letters. Bedad, it is too big for literature itself. You won't get it on paper. You can get little bits; yes, and much good they will do you. Almost any one bit, written, is calculated to mislead the innocent. Why? Because, taken by itself, it is essentially untrue. It's only true when seen as it is seen in reality—one chip in a mosaic. Looked at all on its lonesome, it is essentially false.

"Why, if you'll believe me, the Colonel of the battalion next ours borrowed a handkerchief from me to blow his blessed nose with, in the middle of one of the bloodiest little shows that ever was. 'Got a handkerchief to spare,' he said, in a casual sort of way. 'I used mine, tying up a fellow's arm, back there.' I gave him my handkerchief, he blew his nose comfortably, and shoved the rag in his breeches pocket. 'That's better,' says he, and hurried on with the advance. He was with the rear company of his battalion,

DESCRIBING INDESCRIBABLE 53

and the way he managed to get in and out among his men, cheering them on, was wonderful. He was rather badly wounded later on, in hand-to-hand fighting with four Boches who had cornered two of his men, in their second line. But he's all right, I think. Men were dropping all round us in that advance. It was an extraordinarily bloody business, and had been for thirty hours and more before that. But one remains human, you understand. One tries to get a mouthful of grub at certain intervals, and a smoke if possible. And a man wants to blow his nose on occasion, even though all hell's let loose, and—well, some of us prefer to use handkerchiefs for that purpose, if we can. You follow me. But how easy to convey an entirely false impression, with a picture of a commanding officer borrowing a handkerchief and blowing his nose in the midst of a hot advance.

"Suppose I set out to depict something of the shapeless, grisly horrors of it all. God knows there's enough of 'em. What's the best effect I'll produce, especially on anyone who's never been out there? An effect of shapeless, confused, purposeless horror. Well, is the Push no more than that? You bet it is. Why, looked at from one point of view, it is positively beautiful. From the platoon standpoint it may be a colossal lark or a tangled horror, whilst, from the High Staff standpoint, the main impression may well be one of mathematical nicety, perfectly dovetailed detail, and smooth-working precision. To give you an instance :—

"The other afternoon I came mighty near to puking in a warren of Boche trenches we took outside Longueval. Nothing much. We've all seen worse things. A little heap of four dead Boches. They were decently buried an hour later. It just happened I was about the first of our people to see this particular shambles. You know how careful our chaps are, with their kindly sense of decency. Their first thought is to cover a dead Boche's face, give him some decent dignity, even if they're not able at the moment to give him decent burial. English, Irish, Scots, Canadian, Australian, South African—all the British troops are like that. Well, they hadn't had time to clean up here, and these particular Boches had been done up pretty nasty, as they say, very nasty, indeed. Some of our heavy stuff must have landed right among 'em. They were in the mouth of a dug-out.

"Right. Two minutes later I came upon as homely a little picture as you'd find in the neighbourhood of any peaceful Irish or English village : three of our lads crouching over an old brazier, on which they were making afternoon tea, if you please, frying a scrap of bacon and boiling the water for tea at the same time, and stirring in their own lovable Irish blarney with the cooking all the time. I took it in, and passed on, pondering the queerness of the whole business. I wasn't more than sixty or seventy paces away, when three Boche shells arrived, like a postman's knock, somewhere close behind.

"Two minutes later I came upon as homely a little picture as you'd find in the neighbourhood of any peaceful village."

Just three and no more; one of the flukes of the day.

"Something made me turn back and go to take another look at the tea-party. One of its members had been instantaneously killed, his head smashed to a pulp. Another had been terribly mauled about the loins, and was already being attended to by a couple of stretcher-bearers who had been resting in a dug-out within sight of the party, and themselves had been covered with earth and dust from the shells. I lent a hand, and they very soon had the poor chap on his way down to the dressing station. But I feel sure one won't ever see him again. You know that hopeless yellow pallor. It was ———, of No. 7, and the man killed was ———, of No. 5. I was back that way within a quarter of an hour, and there was ——, of ——'s own section, you know, rolling a cigarette in a bit of newspaper, having just finished the bacon. His half-filled canteen of tea was alongside the brazier, which lay now on its side; upset, no doubt, when the shells came: indeed, it was half buried. But —— told me the bacon had been saved, and, in some queer way, the tea. So he had had ——'s whack and ——'s, as well as his own, and as he rolled his cigarette in the scrap of a Sunday newspaper he was humming ' Keep the home fires burning.'

"My dear Skipper, you can no more hope to get the Push described for folk who haven't been out than you can hope to get the world described, or human life explained, on a postcard. The pen may be ever so mighty, but, believe me, it has its limitations. What's the Push like ? It's like everything that ever was on land or sea, and nothing that ever was as well. It's all the struggles of life crowded into an hour; it's an assertion of the bed-rock decency and goodness of our people, and I wouldn't have missed it, not for all the gold in London town. I don't want to be killed, not a little bit. But, bless you, one simply can't be bothered giving it a thought. The killing of odd individuals such as me is so tiny a matter. My God, Skipper, it's the future of humanity, countless millions, all the laughing little kiddies, and the slim, straight young girls, and the sweet women, and the men that are to come; it's all humanity we're fighting for; whether life's to be clean and decent, free and worth having—or a Boche nightmare. You can't describe it, but I wouldn't like to be out of it for long. It's hell and heaven, and the devil and the world; and, thank goodness, we're on the side of the angels—decency, not material gain—and we're going to win."

CHAPTER V

CLOSE QUARTERS

AMONG those who were permitted to board a certain hospital ship when she berthed at Southampton was Lieut. H——, an officer of the Territorials, whose Battalion accomplished some fine work at Pozières. This officer was sent home during the early part of the Somme offensive, slightly wounded, and will by now have returned to duty. He had not taken half a dozen steps on the vessel's deck before he was saluted by a private of his own Battalion, whose jacket was thickly coated with the grime of later fighting at Pozières, and spattered over with blood, as to its left shoulder. In the powwow that followed one tried to get as accurate a record as possible of this man's own words. This was about the way of it:

"I found your glasses and stick, sir, close to where the stretcher-bearers were hung up that time; you remember, sir, that little dead-end where there had been an old French dug-out. There was a big gas-gong hanging there, you may remember, sir, on the haft of a broken pick in the side of the trench. I gave 'em to Sergeant ——, so they wouldn't be lost. The platoon's in clover now, sir. They were coming out for rest when I was taken away. It was after the Pozières scrappin' was over I got my second wound—getting back down the new sap we made. My first was nothing—machine gun bullet. The platoon's to have two or three days' rest, I believe, sir. Seems queer, resting back there in what used to be the Boche lines, you know, sir. They're ours now, all right, and some of the deep dug-outs are first-rate; came through the crumping all right, they did. That place the ——'s raided, you know, sir, in June it was, when the prisoners started scrappin' on the way back across No Man's Land. You could see our chaps lying about there smokin' and usin' their Tommy's cookers now.

"But we had a hot time all right after you left, sir. The way it was when you left, it went on just the same—not a minute's break—for the rest of the night, all day long, and the next night, before any ease-up came. But Captain —— said the platoon had done real well, sir, what there was left of us. You could see he was pleased, and the Commanding Officer, sir, he said we was a credit to the Regiment; so I think you can feel all right about the platoon, sir. We were moved up to the right—our Company—after you left, and were next the Australians, and I must say they did fight like men, sir; but not any more than our boys. There was a bit of racin', like, between us there, you know, sir, and one of the Anzac corporals told me we made it easy for them; but that must 've been his blarney, sir, because there wasn't nothing easy for anybody in such a hell as that Pozières was.

"I thought at first being dark would make it better for us, but now I think the daylight best. We got to that road at last, you know, sir. It seemed we never could, because of their machine guns; but we did, and the Boche he had it fair honeycombed with deep dug-outs and trenches; but we put the wind up him properly when we got there, sir, my word we did, and those what was left was pretty glad to put their hands up. After the cruel time they'd given us on the slope, our boys did want a mix-up at the end; but Mr. —— and Captain —— they wouldn't have it, sir. They were runnin' up an' down our line tellin' us about it, an' Captain ——, he was near choking for want of breath; but he shouted all he could, and kep' all on putting himself between the Boches with their hands up and us, an' every **one** o they Boches was taken prisoner, and not a one hurt. It's right, too, of course, when they surrender.

"When the order came for our platoon to hold on to that little ridge above where you was hit, sir, I must say I thought it couldn't be done. We was all alone, you know, sir, an' when they tried to bring up another platoon they had to be recalled, for the Boche he had that ground so swep' with his typewriters a swaller couldn't have flown there. Five separate times the Hun came down on us; an' when he wasn't charging he was crumpin' an' machine gunning something chronic. If you lifted your head to look just for a second, you got it in the neck every time. When we got the reinforcement up that night from

No. 8 and No. 7 there was only one of us hadn't been hit; that was little Joey Green, in my section, you know, sir. But we were able to keep the Lewis gun going when they were charging. I think that's what saved us, really, sir. Couldn't use it, only when they was charging, or it would ha' bin blown out of action in a second. But we peppered 'em all right when their fire lifted to let 'em charge. A good little gun, sir, though it did get red-hot. I tell you, sir, I felt like blessin' the chaps who made it so's it could stick the job, an' the chaps that fired it, too, when they'd been pretty badly wounded.

" You see, sir, we was all right with the baynit, so long as it was only maybe two Boches for each of us when they charged. We could manage that pretty comfortable. But if it hadn't bin for the Lewis I think we'd have had half a dozen Boches to each one of us every time he charged; and I don't think we could 've stood it. I had a little parapet of three of 'em, head to tail, in front of me, and I reckon that sheltered me quite a lot. I've got their three caps and baynit sheaths here, that I tied on the back of me belt.

"The fifth time the Boche charged I stopped one with a bullet just before he could reach my baynit, and the one behind him threw down his rifle an' shouted 'Mercy!' with his hands over his head. I wouldn't have hurt him; didn't want to hurt the beggar, you know, sir; though you'd be pretty sick to see one of our boys do the like o' that. But it seemed he couldn't help himself, an' he ran right on to my baynit; spitted himself, he did; I did my very best to patch up the last one; but it was no go, he snuffed it, sir, while I was fixing my field dressing on him. I felt sorry for that Boche, in a way, seein' I hadn't wanted to hurt him at all. I suppose they can't help bein' different from our chaps, ' Mercy, Kamerad ! ' an' all that."

And here is another little story of a private soldier who did his bit on the left of Pozières. A company quartermaster-sergeant, who was wounded by a stray bullet at a ration dump well behind the lines, gave me a note for an officer now in hospital in London. I found out what hospital he was in from the R.A.M.C. staff, and wired asking permission for the publication of the note I was sending him. His reply was: "Anything you like that will do justice to as fine a lot of men as any officer ever had." Well, I don't think this little note does them any injustice, anyhow.

"I am bringing you the wristlet watch that was on ——'s wrist, because the other batmen told me it was yours, and only lent to ——. As I am told you are somewhere in London, sir, I daresay you may be seeing his family. He was with the front line on the left of Pozières, with the rest of his platoon. His mates tell me his rifle had been knocked out of his hand. The shell-holes there must have been hard to cross at the double, in the dark, with such a heavy fire on, too. But —— somehow managed to down his man all right. When they found him he had a Boche's bayonet and rifle in his right hand and his left hand was at the throat of the Boche he'd killed. He was lying right across the man, and he had a bullet through his head. We think a machine gun bullet got him while he struggled with the Boche on the ground, after sticking him with his own bayonet. So you see, sir, your batman died pretty game, like the rest of our boys who went West. But I am glad to say our casualties have been pretty light on the whole, when you think of the masses of Boche dead, not to mention the prisoners. I hear the Brigadier is very pleased indeed with the Battalion's work, and that many in our Company will be mentioned in dispatches. The Sergeant-Major sent his best respects, and hopes your wound is healing well. We have been doing fine lately in the matter of boots and socks, and the rations and bath arrangements have been going like clockwork since you had it out with ———, sir."

CHAPTER VI

THE DEVIL'S WOOD

"No; don't know anything about Pozières. We're from Delville Wood, all three of us. Oh, I don't know. There may have been worse places, you know; but it was a pretty hot shop when we were there; not exactly a health resort, you know, anyhow. If Pozières was worse it must have been quite nasty."

They were all three walking cases, seated at that moment in the companion of the Red Cross ship just berthed. Their bandages were clean, and I have no doubt their wounds were also clean; but for the rest, all that was visible of those three subalterns was —— Well, it had too much of Delville Wood about it to be clean. One feels that some of these tattered, blood-and-soil-stained uniforms should be preserved precisely as they are when their wearers step ashore at Southampton. No doubt some will be. Proud mothers and sisters should see to it. Delville Wood, for example—one example among many—will remain a tremendous memory for a good many of our heroes of all ranks; and, too, a marked point in history.

" I did get one cigarette, or half of it, as a matter of fact, in Devil's Wood," said the fair-haired subaltern whose bloody tunic had been holed over the right shoulder-blade, as well as slashed to

THE DEVIL'S WOOD 75

ribbons in front. " But that was a fluke. I was in quite a deep hole then. You remember that place, ———, just below the left drive. Mostly, the only way to get a moment's comfort in Devil's Wood was to get out of it, dead or alive; and there were times when you felt it didn't much matter which."

"Oh, I say, come off!" protested the dark boy, who, after a course of Turkish baths, might have posed for an artist specialising in cherubic choristers. "It was never so bad as all that, sir. It's rather good to have something to chew in a place like that. Seems to mitigate the stinks, too. I had milk tablets; jolly good things."

"It did niff a bit, didn't it?" said number three. "Always used to think dead

Boches were the most satisfactory kind of Huns; never thought one could see too many. But there were rather too many in Delville. Must say I didn't like 'em; 'specially at night, when a fellow was crawling about. Flies, too; there were more flies than one really wanted in Delville."

"Oh, damn! I hate those flies. One was always thinking about what they'd lit on last."

"Really? Did it strike you that way? I can't say I had much time for thinking about the beggars. But I noticed they were a bit thick. Flies like blood, you know."

"Do they? Well, Delville Wood's the place for 'em, then. Plenty blood there—my aunt! I saw Boches there bled white; the ground all round 'em soaked."

"There's a good deal of solid comfort in a Lewis, if you can find a decent shell-hole handy."

"Hmph! Our own, too. By God! that northern strip was a hot shop. How many machine guns do you reckon the Boche had there? Like a typewriting shop, wasn't it?"

"But it was rather jolly when Fatty got our little Lewis up in front there, wasn't it? Made the rifles seem a bit slow. There's a good deal of solid comfort in a Lewis, you know, if you can find a decent shell-hole handy. I liked the red spit of it in the night. Pretty comforting that when you heard the Boches creeping."

"That was one of the things about the Wood; you never could move in it without making some row."

"Row! But did you ever hear anything like the row our heavies made in that last hurricane burst? I was trying to explain to my sergeant just what we were going to do, when the curtain lifted, and, 'pon my word, though I yelled in his ear, he couldn't hear me."

" Fine, that, wasn't it ? the scramble when it lifted. God! it was a great fight, that last bit. Our chaps had their teeth set then, all right. One of my section commanders was wounded in three places before we started; but he went like an absolute madman in that scramble up the little ridge. Never saw anything like it in my life. His face was covered with blood, he'd got no coat, and his shirt had been all torn away in putting field dressings on him. Nobody could keep up with him. I tried hard, but he got ahead of me, and he downed two big Boches in that shallow trench as though they'd been thistles—just smothered them, he did; and then—then he got it fairly in the neck. Bomb burst right at his feet; laid out three other chaps at the same time. He was a man, that chap. I got a bit of his own back for him. It was a Boche sergeant shied that bomb at ——; but he'll never throw another. I beg pardon. No, no; I hadn't got a rifle then. But I had my little truncheon though, and it was good enough. Oh, I don't think he was the surrendering kind. Anyway, he didn't get the chance. —— was one of my own section commanders, you see, and one of the best. Yes, I made quite sure about that particular Boche. He wasn't a bad sort; put up a good enough fight."

"Aye, aye, a queer business. You know there were some real brave things done at the end of that show. They can't give D.C.M.'s to everyone, you know; but, honestly, all those men earned it, just as well as any of the chaps who get it."

"Of course they did. So do thousands every day in this Push. Thousands of 'em every day are doing bigger, finer things than lots of things men got the V.C. for in the old days."

(The "old days" are, of course, the days before '14, to these young veterans—God bless them!)

"Yes, but look here; what I was thinking of was the lot of things that nobody at all ever knows about; not even a man's own mates. Now, look here. You know we had to fall back a bit, once, from that shallow trench at the top. No, I mean after we'd been in it, and thought we'd got it. Yes. Well, we fell back for—oh, it must 've been ten minutes, the time I mean, and a lot more Boches came up along those communicating saps, and it almost looked once as though we wouldn't get it back again."

"Never looked any other way, I thought. Can't for the life of me see how the devil we ever did get it. Damn it! It was obviously impossible to get it, because of those machine guns."

"I know. Well, I got my dose in the trench, you know. When I saw you all falling back I tried like the devil to get out. I was in quite a deep bit, alongside that traverse with the big tree on it, where —— was killed. I nearly broke blood-vessels trying to get out; but it was no go. My shoulder was giving me hell, and the right arm wouldn't work at all. Well, you know, I'd rather have been sent West altogether. I always did feel I'd rather anything than be taken by the Boches. I had my revolver, of course; but I'm not much good with my left hand. Ten to one they'd have got me alive.

"I could just see over the edge, and I was cursing my luck, when I saw a chap deliberately stop, turn round and look at me, and sort of weigh up his chances. He was falling back with the rest of our lot, you know. Just then a Boche machine gun opened as it seemed right alongside me. It was really just round the big traverse. 'That settles it,' I thought. 'I'm done now.' And it did settle it, too. That chap I'd seen, who'd evidently decided once that it wasn't good enough, he altered his mind when the typewriter began. Down on his hands and knees he went, and scuttled all the way back to where I was, like a lizard. He fairly gasped at me; no breath, you know.

" 'On me back, sir,' says he.

"And, somehow, he hauled me out and slung me over his back. I fell off three separate times while he was scrambling down the slope with me, and three separate times he stopped, in all that fire, and fixed me up again. And then I felt him crumple up under me, and at the same time I got—this; through the

left arm. I rolled clear and looked at
his face. I'll never forget his face, but
he had no coat or cap, and I didn't
know his battalion. His forehead was
laid open and bleeding fast. I dragged him
behind a stump and laid him with his
head on my haversack. Then I scrambled
out to find a stretcher-bearer for him.
But I got caught up in our advance
then. You know what it is. And I went
on, thinking I'd find my man after. Glad
I went in a way, because I had three
bombs a wounded corporal gave me,
and it was easy lobbing them with my
left at close quarters. By gad, I lobbed
'em all right; nearly lobbed myself to
Kingdom come, too. But those bombs
did their job all right, before we cleared
the trench. It was hours after, before I

could get a man to help me look for that good chap who'd dragged me out, and we never found him—never a sign of him. But to do what he did, thinking it out, too, in all that hell—why, many a chap's got the V.C. for no more than that, I think."

" Yes, and there were dozens of things like that in Delville alone."

" Same all along the front."

" Right through the Push."

" I believe it is, 'pon me word."

" I'm dead sure of it."

" Oh, I tell you, as the men say : ' The Army of to-day's all *right* ! ' "

" London train ? Yes, that's me, orderly. Come on, boys. I beg your pardon ! Good-bye, sir ! "

CHAPTER VII

THE COCKNEY FIGHTER

AMONG the wounded who arrived recently at Southampton one found both officers and men whose experiences since July 1st may be described as unique in all the world's history of war. These are men who " went over the sticks " at 7.30 a.m. on July 1st, and have been fighting at one point or another in the present great offensive north of the Somme ever since.

There are, of course, magnificent soldiers in the French Army who have been through an even longer period of fighting at Verdun; and the fighting before

Verdun was probably the most intense recorded in history up to that time. But, as a French officer stated only the other day, after returning wounded from the south of Péronne : " The British part in the Somme offensive has been Verdun magnified, Verdun on a bigger scale." Another French officer has stated that the artillery fire in some portions of this line has been " more terrible, more intense, more devastating than the worst seen at Verdun."

When one carefully thinks out what the day-to-day and night-to-night fighting has been between Authille and Guillemont since July 1st, and then comes to talk to a soldier who has actually been through the whole of it, one marvels that any ordinary twentieth century human being could possibly survive such a month so spent. One talked with many, on the landing stage, who not only have survived it, but can jest about it, and talk with indomitable cheeriness about getting back to it " before the show's over." Pte. A—— ——, of the —th ——, will retain always a prominent place in my gallery of such wounded heroes, who have not the faintest notion that there is anything heroic about them. He is a Cockney of the Cockneys. I have met his like in the ranks of the old Army, the Territorials, and the New Armies; but never, certainly, one who has known such months as Pte. A—— has just lived through; never before this year.

" Fed up? Wot, ahr boys fed up, sir? Not likely! Wy, we're just beginnin'

THE COCKNEY FIGHTER

to like it. But I bet Mister Boche is gettin' a bit fed up. Least, some er them as I saw, they was; right up to the bloomin' neck, as ye might say, sir."

But I feel there is something terribly inadequate about my attempt to reproduce Pte. A——'s *rycy* vernacular; also I cannot hope to convey on paper any conception of the incorrigibly humorous devilry in the man's mobile face. Brave! I would say he was braver than a stoat; and that may mean something to anyone who has known a stoat defy him and his stick on a footpath; who has been deliberately challenged, as I have been, to mortal combat with a stoat over the body of a crippled field mouse. Pte. A—— got his quietus in Delville Wood. Three separate times before, after July 1st, he was slightly wounded, and received all the attention he would accept at advanced field dressing stations. In Delville Wood he went on fighting for a long time with considerable wounds in left shoulder and arm, and only gave out when rendered perfectly helpless by a smashed ankle and two slight head wounds.

"To 'ear the wy they talks abaht that Devil's Wood you'd think there wuz something *wrong* abaht the bloomin' plice. Fer me, I like the in-an'-aht close work, I do; better'n this bloomin' extended order work in the open, wiv the bloomin' typewriters clack-clackin' till you carn't 'ear yourself speak. An' they carn't 'ardly 'elp hittin' of yer, neither. Same's it was at Monterbang an' comin' up to Longyval. No, give me the in-an'-aht work, I

"He went on fighting for a long time with considerable wounds in his left shoulder."

sy, every time. You do git a bit er fun fer yer money in a plice like Devil's Wood. I've done a bit er scrappin' down at Wonderland, I 'ave, an' when my orficer give me a little trench dagger, wot fitted on me left 'and like a knuckle-duster—'e 'ad two er three of 'em, 'e 'ad—wy, I tell you, it was a little bit uv orlright fer me.

"There's suthin' to keep a man amused abaht that sorter fighting. Not like this open order work, where you never knows 'oo 'its yer. I didn't arf walk into them Boches when we rushed 'em in the Wood; not arf, I didn't. 'Time, genelmen!' I useter sy. Much I cared abaht their toastin' forks once I could git close in. You let me get close in, sir, same's we did in Devil's Wood, time an' time again, an'

I'll back meself to serve ye up Boches fast as you can open oysters.

" No, I've got no fault to find with Devil's Wood. If only a R.E. fatigue party could er got in there first an' done a bit uv a clean up, as ye might say; got some uv the wood an' wire an' rubbish an' that outer the wy, an' jest levelled it up er bit—wy, you couldn't 've asked fer a nicer plice fer a scrap.

" Wot do I think uv Mister Boche ? Oh, 'e's orlright once yer get ter know 'is little tricks—the blighter. 'E's got some toler'bly dirty little tricks; but 'e's a sticker, ye know, sir. Yuss, 'e's a sticker, orlright, 'specially with a machine gun. 'E don't count once you can land 'im one on the point er the jaw. The sight o' steel makes 'im proper sick.

You gotter be quick as a flash once you get up to 'im, or 'e'll up with 'is 'ands, an' then you mustn't touch the beggar, although you know bloomin' well that if you 'appen to stumble, or give 'im arf a charnce, 'e'll stick yer when you're not looking—almost the only time 'e will, that is. But 'e's a pretty good soldier at shootin' ranges.

"The Push? Oh, the Push is orlright, sir. Tike er bit er time, ye know, to flatten 'im out proper; but 'e's goin' to be flattened orlright; not arf, 'e ain't Did I get any sleep last month? Lor' bless ye, yes, sir. I can't get on wivout me sleep. We used to doss it in shell-holes; any ole plice. Soon get used to that. 'Ad me tea, too, most arternoons, I did. Bit uv a relish with it, too, when we'd got in a Boche trench. I'll say that fer the Boches, their dug-outs is prime. Gen'rally always find a bit er suthin' tasty in a Boche dug-out, an' if yer strike a orficer's dug-out it's a Lord Mayor's banquit fer certin."

It is impossible for me to begin to do justice to Pte. A—— on paper. I wish he could meet some of our literary masters of Cockney humour, for, though what I am able to quote may but faintly indicate it, men like this are perfectly wonderful in their attitude toward the great things they have seen and done. This man—who is only one among thousands—has moved and lived and had his hourly being night and day for many weeks past in a nearer approach to the old writers' dreams of hell than anything

THE COCKNEY FIGHTER 95

ever previously seen on earth. Not for an hour in all that time has he been out of reach of gun-fire, or away from the maniacal din, the murderous fury of it all. He is now pretty badly cut about, and has lost a lot of blood. But he hardly ever opens his mouth without emitting a jest of some kind; he talks cheerily of getting back into the inferno, and very probably will be back there before very many weeks have passed. As for Delville, which several officers have told me was the most awful and bloody shambles of the whole terrific series, he says that bar its untidiness, so to say, " you couldn't 've asked fer a nicer plice fer a scrap ! "

If the Kaiser could produce many such soldiers as this one—well, the war would last a very long time. Myself, I greatly doubt if the All Highest could produce one such among all his legions. And I have talked with many scores of just this type, and hundreds of other types as fine in their different ways, during the past few weeks alone.

It is to be remembered always that this is the spirit they show when wounded, and straight from the most exhausting kind of fighting ever seen, and a long tiring journey. Heaven help the Hun who meets them when, with all the knowledge they have gleaned of his little ways, they re-enter the fight at the end of comfortable weeks of good living and recuperation!

CHAPTER VIII

" WE DON'T COUNT WOUNDS IN MY REGIMENT "

STANDING close beside the gangway of the first hospital ship to be berthed at Southampton during one recent day was a tall, fair-haired sergeant, who came to attention and saluted, like a guardsman on parade, though his left arm was slung and his tunic in tatters. The dust which covered his ragged jacket was caked on it, by darker, thicker stuff than water: the familiar, unmistakable stain which covers so much khaki on hospital ships; the stain that tells you a man has given freely of the life within him in the service of King and country.

There was nothing in these details to hold one's attention to the sergeant; for these are external characteristics shared by most of our new arrivals at Southampton. But in some indescribable way the sergeant was trim and smart, though bandaged and clothed in rags that were muddy and bloody. His smartness, then, must have gone a good way beneath the surface. It certainly was marked. I waited a few minutes to chat with this N.C.O., and it happened that the first question I put to him took this form :—

" Well, Sergeant, how do you think the New Army is shaping ? "

There was something at once humorous,

modest, and very pleasing about his flickering half-smile.

"The New Army, sir? Oh, I think the New Army's all right, sir. Doing fine, I should say. Master Boche finds 'em a pretty tough nut to crack, I think. I don't think there's much the matter with the New Army, sir, from the little I've seen of it."

"Why, haven't you been out long, then, Sergeant?"

Again that flickering, modest, humorous smile.

"I was in the retreat from Mons, sir; wounded there, and hit again at Loos, sir. This is my third trip home in a hospital ship. But, of course, it's all different now."

"Then you are of the old Army?"

"Fourteen years' service, sir, come next month."

"H'm! When you come out of hospital this time you'll wear three gold stripes, sergeant."

The smile was perfectly radiant this time.

"We don't count wounds in my Regiment, sir."

It would be most difficult to explain how much this sergeant impressed me, or what was conveyed by his smile and his tone. There was, for example, a kind of caress in his voice when he used those two simple words "my Regiment," which I am quite sure cannot be described.

Some hours later, on another ship, I had some little talk about it with an officer of the Regular Army, a captain whose majority cannot be far from him, I apprehend. He has seen service in Gallipoli, as well as in France, and been wounded in both theatres of war.

"Odd you should mention that," he said. "I've been thinking of that very point: the New Army and the Old. I put in two days and a night at Havre, you know, on the way from the front, and some kind soul has supplied the place I was in with stacks of newspapers. I read papers of every day for a month; all about the present offensive. I was awfully glad to see the public have been getting lots of information about the way the Service Battalions have distinguished themselves. I think they deserve every word of praise they've got, and more. They really are wonderful. It's a great achievement for men to be so steady in attack, after so short a training. Their officers have done splendidly, too, and it's good that the public at home should learn something about it. I very much doubt if any other country in the world could have accomplished anything approaching to it, in the time. Tradition counts for an enormous deal, you see, in any army; in the training and the fighting men make soldiers of one another, you know, given the tradition and the atmosphere. And in the absence of these things to have accomplished what this country has accomplished in the New Army—well, it's a wonderful tribute to the qualities of the race. Nobody knows so well as a regular soldier what a wonderful miracle it is."

"WE DON'T COUNT WOUNDS" 103

I forget just how my next question was worded, but I know it provoked frank and hearty laughter from the captain.

"Oh, Lord, no!" he said. "No need to tell the public about the Regulars. They don't need any telling about regiments that have been fighting in different parts of the world for centuries. The world hardly wants telling at this time of day that Tommy is an invincibly fine soldier—the very best. He proved it such a long time ago, and he's been proving it ever since. But it's only right that our people should be given all the facts about the New Army. It had to prove itself; and, begad, it's done it magnificently. I don't think there can be a shadow of doubt about that. But I do think it's only right and fair that the facts which prove it should be made public. Everybody who's been in the show knows it; but the world ought to know it, too. As for us—well, they know all about us, don't they?

"Of course, it's a mistake to suppose that we have two separate fighting forces— Old Army and New Army. It isn't that at all. The Service Battalions, as you know, are mostly battalions of regiments whose records were fine records before the German Empire was ever thought of. Some of 'em have been lucky enough to get a certain number of Regular N.C.O.'s, and some a few Regular officers. Some have been luckier than others in the matter of the number of ex-Regulars they got in their ranks. Those things are a great help, of course, in the training,

The old regular senior N.C.O. is a finely finished production.

as well as in the campaign. The old Regular senior N.C.O. or warrant officer is a finely finished production, as you know; a pretty valuable centre of influence. There are battalions and companies in the New Army that owe an enormous deal to a single Regular sergeant-major, and there are Service battalions with retired Regular officers commanding, whose training has made them equal to any line battalion in the world.

"Then, of course, there are plenty of Regular battalions with hardly a score of the old hands left in the ranks. They have done their bit from first to last, and done it so well that they have had to be remade many times over from drafts. But the Regiment never dies, you know. The root of the matter is there all the time, and the surviving officers and N.C.O.'s work pretty hard to prevent any falling off in its quality. I think, perhaps, that's really the whole thing, isn't it? A strictly non-military nation has, in an extraordinarily short space of time, built up a huge Army from the very closely pollarded stem of a little one which—well, perhaps the arch-Hun did make a bit of a mistake when he described it as 'contemptible' as well as little. Its record wasn't exactly contemptible, was it? The root is the old root, and the present big tree seems to me to have the old fibre running all through it. Can't very well give it higher praise, can you? And, mind you, it deserves the highest praise that can be given, as I think the Boche is beginning to realise."

CHAPTER IX

A REVEREND CORPORAL

THE last wounded man I talked with on the landing-stage at Southampton on a certain night was in hospital away up north next morning. His two wounds were both clean and slight, and within a week or so he would, no doubt, be enjoying sick leave in his own Border-country home. Wherever he is, he will, I think, be an influence for good; and—yes, I am sure of it—a greater influence for good than he could have been if he had played no part in this war.

He is a corporal now, and his name

was in his battalion orderly room for a lance-sergeant's stripes when he stopped the bullets that gave him his break for rest and recuperation in Blighty. Up till some time early in 1915 he was a minister of the Gospel, newly ordained. When the end of the war comes he will resume his sacred calling, and one would like to hear him preach. I am very sure he will not have lost anything as preacher, teacher, or minister by his service in another capacity. A man does not lose by the teaching of discipline and the experience of shoulder-to-shoulder comradeship in the trenches with men who voluntarily offer their lives in the defence of all that every good man holds sacred.

This corporal's face and neck and hands are of a rich old saddle brown, and his eyes, despite the weariness in them, have a light which it is good to see in the eyes of a man. He knows a very great deal more about many things, including life and British human nature, than he knew eighteen months ago, and he has found it all well worth fighting for; dying for, if need be, as he has seen many of his comrades die.

"I was just north of Ovillers, where the new line joins the old, you know. We are practically at right angles to our old lines there, you know; looking north now instead of east, and in our rear you can walk about and take your ease in the warren that stood for death to us before July 1st. And what a warren! Round about Ovillers and La Boiselle, I mean. It's marvellous to think those lines could ever have been taken. I am not a bit surprised the Hun thought them impregnable. Anyone would, when you come to look over them. Even now, when they have been pounded out of all recognition by our heavies, you'd think such a network could be held against any possible advance. The Boche thinks the same about Thiépval, you know; that no power on earth will ever take it from him, because he's made a fortified arsenal of it. But there's a force behind our chaps that he can never have in this war, and I doubt if his generals make any allowance for that.

"And yet, you know, that force, whatever you like to call it, will presently smash Thiépval just as surely as it smashed Ovillers and La Boiselle and the other

"There's a force behind our chaps that the Boche will never have in this war."

impregnable strong points. I'm no expert, of course; but it seems queer to me that these highly trained people who run the Boche machine should show the ignorance they do of everything they can't weigh and measure and touch with their fingers. It's been the same all through the war, from the very first outrage in Belgium. So far, the Boche would seem to be incapable of grasping the existence of anything that cannot be turned out of a foundry.

"Of course I know the foundry has played a tremendous part in the war, and I know the bravest heart can't go on beating after you've smashed it with a Boche shell. But that doesn't alter my point, really. Shells alone would, I think, have left places like La Boiselle and

Ovillers what the Boche thought them: impregnable. But behind and over and above our shells—without which we can, I know, do nothing—our fellows have something which the Boches have not got in this war, or in their nation as at present constituted, and, believe me, it's that something that's winning the war for us and our Allies.

"Oh, I'm no authority, of course. But, just as it's their job to know all about tactics and munitions, so it was mine, and is, to know a little about men's souls or spirits; to try hard to learn about them, anyhow; to study them all I can. I've been studying more closely since I 'joined up' than I ever did before, and the study has brought me two certainties, that the German Army and the German nation have set themselves a perfectly hopeless task, and that they cannot possibly prevail against us, and that the Allies will presently beat the Germans absolutely to a standstill, more than anything else because of elements at work on our side which Germany does not recognise or understand, and of which her magnificent organisation has taken no account at all.

"Am I preaching? Forgive me. It boils down to this: their machinery for destroying our flesh and bones is pretty good, though I think we have mastered that this year, thanks to our unarmed armies in the home workshops. But they have devised nothing adequate to put up against the spirit of our armies in the field; nothing adequate at all. And yet, mark my words, that it is that is going to carry us through their lines. It's that that is going to enable me to smoke my pipe in the midst of their fortified arsenal at Thiépval when I get back. I'm just as certain of it as I am that I smoked a pipe the night before I was hit, in the middle of what, in June, was such an utterly deadly place for us as the chalky trench walls beyond Mash Valley, between Ovillers and La Boiselle."

Whether or not there was logic in his words, there was a conviction behind them which I found most compelling. (That is one reason why I want to hear this corporal preach after the war.) I asked for further details as to this asset of ours against which the Hun has made no provision. "Tell me what this spirit is," I asked.

"Ah! I'm afraid I can't do that. I'm not so very sure that anyone could. You can't measure it, remember; and it's not made in factories. It would be so easy to use words that would mislead you, words that might mean one thing for me and another for you. And I don't really think that any words could do justice to it, anyhow. It is there, all right, I can assure you. Men cannot march smilingly into certain death with a cheer on their lips without it. Specially primed men may be driven anywhere, as we have seen Boches driven; but our chaps are not primed, and never driven. Yet the Boche cannot make them waver.

"No, it is beyond me to describe it. I think, perhaps, one must live among our fellows in the trenches to understand it rightly. Our officers know all about it. The Boche fights because he's got to fight. Our chaps fight because—well, the fact that as soldiers they have got to fight is the least of the things that make them fight. For one thing, they know as well as I do that we are going to win. They came forward voluntarily to fight, because they know we ought to win; and that for our sort of people, for people holding the sort of beliefs the British people hold, life wouldn't be worth living, ever, if we didn't win.

"But I feel that the words I am using are quite futile—such little shadows beside the thing itself. I fancy the public will get as near understanding it as anybody can without living in the trenches and seeing the spirit at work among the men, if they just think carefully over what our men have been going through on that front, what they have been doing since July and how they have done it—cheering, singing, shouting—how gladly they have done it. Then let the public ask themselves how and why. The most of the men of the New Armies have no military tradition behind them; had never handled a gun till they 'joined up.' Yet they have faced bigger things than any veterans ever faced before, and faced them steadily; ah, so steadily; seeing it all very clearly, and fearing it not one scrap, though they have forced mad fear into the highly trained troops facing them again and again. That is because they have something that you cannot make in foundries; that you cannot even give by training. Words won't explain it, but quiet thought may. I could give it a name the Church would recognise. But let's just say they know their cause is good, as they very surely do. The Germans may write on their badges that God is with them, but our lads—they *know*."

CHAPTER X

BROTHERS OF THE PARSONAGE

THERE have been busy phases of the day's work at Southampton, when two of the green and white hospital ships have been lying alongside the stage together, both with full passenger lists of wounded from the Somme. On one such occasion the living freight of the smaller boat was still being discharged when I went on board the big one. There one was talking with one of the cot cases, whose foot had been rather badly knocked about by a German bomb. In his pleasure in the fact that it was his foot, and not his head, which caught the more malevolent portions of that particular bomb, Lieut. R—— seemed to think it was rather an advantage than otherwise to lose a toe or two. "Nothing to write home about, anyhow," was his way of putting it.

One had occasion to ask his name, this high-spirited fellow who thought himself so extraordinarily lucky to have nothing more than a temporarily smashed foot. And then I turned back to another page of my note-book.

"Why, there's another man of your name," I said, "on board the ——, lying just astern here."

"You don't mean to say it's Teddy?"

"Don't know, I'm sure. Here's the name, look, Second-Lieut. E. S. R——, of the —th ——s."

"Well, I'll be jiggered if it isn't Teddy. I say—you must excuse me, you know; but that's my elder brother. He must have been in this show, too. They only came out about Christmas time, you know, and I never knew where his brigade was. How was he hit? How is he? Is he a cot case or a walker? How'd he seem? Does he look all right? What an extraordinary lark! Fancy Teddy being—what?"

Five minutes later one had secured permission from the kindly R.A.M.C. Staff Officer for "Teddy"—the senior in years was the junior in rank, I noticed—to leave his ship and come on board the other vessel till his train was ready. It was rather pleasant to watch the meeting of the two brothers who had been in

France for eight months without either knowing precisely where the other was. "Teddy" was a "walking case" as it happened, so that there was no difficulty about his getting to his brother. He had been hit when fighting beside the Bapaume road, close to Pozières; his brother, on the terrible northern slopes of Delville Wood, above Longueval.

One rather wished one had a phonograph in which to record some of the talk that passed between these two sons of an English country parson who had last met, during their training period in 1915, in a sequestered south-country rectory, and had since lived through many months of strenuous trench warfare, and some weeks of such strife as the world has never seen before, all between the Ancre and the Somme.

Both have known winter in waterlogged trenches and abysmal mud; both have gasped and spat from the choking thirst that comes to a fighting man during July and August heats on a chalky soil, when he struggles in blinding dust and dense choking smoke over ground which has been pulverised in almost every yard of it by bursting high explosive and rending steel. They had a good deal to say, and some of it was not very coherent or easy for the outsider to follow; both were in the same tearingly high spirits. Men wounded and broken in the war! It was hard to believe it, as one watched their sparkling eyes and the constant flash of white teeth against dark, sunburnt skin, while they laughed in sheer gaiety of heart. Wounded, perhaps, and one felt that would not affect them for long; but these English lads are not so easily broken. There is a good deal of the born fighter in them, despite our non-military traditions; and, for one who knows the trenches in northern France, it is striking evidence of enduring virility and invincible good-heartedness to find men so amazingly debonair, and in the towering spirits of holiday schoolboys, after eight or nine months spent in the fighting line between Fricourt and Arras.

This is a specimen of the sort of verbal battledore and shuttlecock which went on between the junior superior officer in the cot and the senior of lower rank who was a " walking case."

"Fancy you, you secretive old beggar, being here, and I never even knew you were in the show."

"Well, what about you, if you come to that. You got it in the foot, eh? What is it—shrap?"

"No, bomb. Yours in the arm—you old blighter?"

"Shoulder; in up here, near the collar-bone, and out through the shoulder-blade. Machine gun bullet; clean as can be. I'll be clear in a week or two. What the deuce d'you want to get a bomb in the foot for? What were you doing?"

"I was jolly lucky, I can tell you. We were rushing their last trench in the Delville Wood; weren't more than a dozen paces in front of it. I fell, regular somersault, in a shell-hole, at the very moment one of their bombs went off right alongside me. Head down in the hole, safe, you see; heels up, and one of 'em got caught. But my orderly got the Boche who shied it; got him for keeps, I can tell you. First Boche he'd killed, I think, and, begad, he made no end of a mess of the chap. Insisted on giving me the fellow's helmet. Here it is, look; though, as I told him, it was more up to me to be giving him something. He seemed to think it was a gross kind of insubordination for the Boche to have shied a bomb at his officer. Nice boy. Mother keeps a little shop of sorts in ———. We must get the mater to look her up. So you were up there by Pozières?"

"A bit south-west of it."

" Hot stuff, wasn't it—Pozières ? "

" So so; not a rest cure, you know. I've got a helmet, too; but I can beat you, me boy. Mine's an officer's—a real live Boche officer; least, he was live enough then, with a sword-stick of all things, and I've got his sword-stick, too."

" No, Teddy ! What a lark ! Did you really get the beggar ? "

" Well, he got me first; punctured my left hand here, you see. I'd lost my revolver long before; but I'd got a Boche rifle and bayonet—pretty good one, too. You'd have laughed to see the duel; like a Naval and Military Tournament show, you know—sword *versus* bayonet. I daresay he was a swordsman. Lots of these Huns are, you know. If so, I 'spect my ignorance of the game put him off. I simply rushed him, you know; got him clean through the chest. Queer thing! He was the only Boche officer I've seen, and we've been in front ever since the 1st."

"I know. They've been lying remarkably doggo. Getting a bit short, I suppose—else they've lost their appetite. How'd your men do?"

"Finest platoon in the New Army bar none!"

"Oh, come; I swear they're not that; can't be. I've got the best; everyone in our lot knows that. But yours were good, were they?"

"Good! my dear chap, there isn't a man in the platoon that oughtn't to have the V.C.; not a blessed one."

"H'm! So yours were the same, eh?

Mine were absolutely perfect. I knew they were fine, but honestly I'd no idea how fine till we got into Delville. Honest Injun, a man can't help loving 'em."

" I know. It's queer, isn't it? the way you feel that. You really can't help loving 'em—dammem! Seen the papers ? "

" Saw some last night. All this business about the third year, and Big Willie trying to keep their spirits up. Notice the way the Boches try to make little of the Push. We've gained such a few miles, they say. Pretty useful miles, though, to the top of the ridge."

" Oh, besides; it's not only the ground, you know. See what it really means. They've taught their people the English couldn't really stand against 'em, let alone advance. How could we advance even one mile on selected ground they wanted so badly, and get thousands of 'em prisoners, and regular piles of 'em dead—if we were so contemptible? They'll find it hard to go on pumping in the same kind of tosh to any of their troops that have been in this show. Never get them to believe it any more."

"No, by Jove! They'll go on fighting, of course. They jolly well can't help that. And their a'tillery and machine guns will go on playing merry hell, no doubt; but I think the wind's up 'em; I do really, Teddy. I know it was at Delville; fairly up 'em."

One slipped away at about that stage and had a little talk with some of the kindly R.A.M.C. people, with the result

BROTHERS OF THE PARSONAGE 131

that the brothers did not go away by different trains, but were booked for the same hospital, which I hope they will very soon leave together, for a few weeks of holiday recuperation in the south-country rectory. Our Army is full of lads like these, and their quality is super-excellent.

CHAPTER XI

THE AUSTRALIAN AS A FIGHTER

"I THINK this must be my month for doing it, sir—August," said a Company Sergeant-Major of the —th ——s, whom one found enjoying a cigarette in his cot on board one of the hospital ships at Southampton. The upper part of his face and head were all hidden in white bandages, and he had had a machine gun bullet through the upper part of his left leg; but he was—"Doing very nicely now, thank you," and in first-rate spirits, both over the prospect of a few weeks' holiday at home—that is how he regards it—and with regard to the outlook at the front.

"When the war's over I shall have my hands full every August with celebrations. I joined up on August 15th, 1914, went to France on August 2nd, 1915, was knocked out near Bazentin on August 2nd, 1916, and born on August 3rd, 1884. Certainly must be my month for doing it, sir, mustn't it?

"I think the Boche will be a long time before he forgets August, 1916, sir, or July, either. Don't think he likes our boys when they've got their tails fairly up, the way they have now. He's all right at a comfortable distance, when he's got things his own way, is Master Boche; but he don't like it a little bit when our chaps get right in among his lot, the way they're doing now. He don't like that, sir; not a little bit. With rifles, machine guns, heavies, trench mortars, rifle grenades, minnenwerfers, and all the like o' that, he's just as happy as the day is long. He can go on at that game till the cows come home, and I'm not saying but what he's mighty good at it. He is, you know, sir. And what with his fine dug-outs, an' one thing with another, he can stand a whole lot of it from us, too, an' not be very much the worse for it. But he do not like close quarters, sir, and he won't stick it, that's the next thing.

"I reckon, if they could arrange for this war to be decided by one good fight between a Boche battalion and a British, in one open field with never a hole or a trench in it, the war would be over in twenty minutes, and there wouldn't be any more of that Boche battalion left; no, not if it was the best they've got in their Prussian Guards. The best of 'em can't stand up to our lads once they get down to real business alongside each other. The trouble is to get near enough, of course. But we'll be there all right before long, now, sir, if we can keep up the munitions supply.

"You see that chap down there in the cot next the ladder, sir, the one speaking to the Sister now, that's him. He's an Australian, he is; comes from a place in New South Wales. His battalion was in the thick of the Pozières show, and they say he's goin' to be given a Commission. I don't know. But I was talking last night to a chap in his platoon who was alongside him in the last fighting there, and he told me there was one traverse that chap got into where the Boches was too thick on the ground, as you might say, for him to work his bayonet. They reckoned they'd got him, of course; goin' to eat him, they was. They'd got his rifle out of his hands; such a jam he couldn't draw back for a thrust, you see. And they'd somehow got him down, when his mate came round the corner of the traverse. He says there were seven of the Boches.

"Well, what his mate saw was just the seven Boches, like in a football scrum, swayin' to an' fro. He couldn't see this chap at all. He was underneath, you see. So this other chap, he just gives one yell an' starts in with his baynit. That made a bit of a break-away, as ye might say, an' after that the fun began. The chap who told me was a little bit of a fellow; couldn't ha' been more'n five feet five, another Australian, a light-weight, he was. He hung on to his baynit, an' put in plenty foot-work, keepin' clear, you see. An' he says the way his mate—the big chap in the cot there—laid them Boches out was the sight of a life-time. He just downed 'em with his hands, an' the chap told me that when he got a Boche down, that Boche was done; he wasn't takin' any more. Anyway, they took two of 'em prisoners, an' they couldn't take the other five because they was dead—dead as mutton. And the fellow told me that big chap did it all with his two hands. He's cut about a bit, you know, and they laid his head open for him, but—one man against seven, you know, an' them all armed! It takes some doin'. The Sister tol' me he'd be all right in a week. They're hot stuff, you know, sir, these Australians, once they get goin'. Our boys the same. They're happy when they get to close quarters, an' that's just what Mister Boche can't stand at no price."

One of the things one notices about ninety per cent. of our wounded is that to get the story of their own personal part in the fighting one has to go to someone else who was with them. They are talkative enough about their mates, but they are given to a modest and wholly lovable reticence regarding their own exploits. This

Company sergeant-major, for instance, who told me about the Australian told me no word of the incident of which an officer of his Company afterwards told me on the landing-stage. Despite his head wounds and a bullet through his upper leg he had carried his wounded Company Commander from a Boche sap into our own line, under a fire which would have made most wounded men think only of lying very low, in any sort of cover they could get.

" There was a private in our Company," said the lieutenant who told me of the sergeant-major's brave act, " fellow named —— ——, who earned the mention in dispatches I am sure he'll presently get if ever a man did. One of these jolly, larky little chaps he is, always turning up at orderly room in the morning when we were training at home—incorrigible chap for the very small misdemeanours, you know—but what a little brick when he's really up against it! The N.C.O.'s of his platoon were knocked out to a man, just north of Bazentin-le-Petit there. Fritz had a machine gun behind a knoll that simply kept us grilling. This little chap, ——, got the balance of the platoon together—fifteen or twenty of 'em, you know—and made a dash for the flank of that knoll. There were only five of 'em got there, I'm sorry to say, and by that time —— had three bullet wounds. But when they got there they just wiped the earth with the Boches at that gun, smothered 'em; and little —— turned the gun on the Boche line and kept it clacking two or three hundred to the minute till I was able to get along there with No. 9

platoon and take over; and he wouldn't have slacked off then, in spite of his wounds, if I hadn't made an order of it—a great little fighter and a born leader, mind you, too. There's lots of his sort on our side, thank goodness!"

CHAPTER XII

NEWS FOR THE O.C. COMPANY AT HOME

It would not be easy to find among the wounded as they arrive men who have recently had any experience of either leisure or comfort. Freedom to rest, to chat, to eat comfortable meals and smoke a pipe at ease, to read a newspaper or to write a letter—all these things have the charm of novelty and are enjoyed with the zest that belongs only to unaccustomed luxuries by our newly arrived wounded officers and men.

"Haven't been able to write a word except my signature on two or three field service post cards since the big push began."

One has heard that remark from a good many of the new-comers. One morning a wounded officer had a rather longer wait between the time of his ship being berthed and his train pulling out than the average.

"It's rather different from waiting in a trench," he said; "I could stand a good deal of this." As a matter of fact he put in most of the time in writing to his Company Commander, who, having been wounded at an early stage in the present offensive, has lain since in a London hospital. From that letter I am permitted to reproduce the following:

"It's no good my attempting to give you any war news, because there in London

I've no doubt you get far more than we do and know more about it; but, as you've been away nearly a month now, I thought you'd like a line or two about the Company. I don't suppose we've appeared in the leading articles yet, have we? Not but what the men of your Company deserve as much space there as any in the Army; I'm jolly sure of that. We've lost nearly half our strength—not killed, I'm glad to say, but wounded—but the spirit of those that are left would do your heart good. I want to tell you one thing particularly.

" You heard about the way the Battalion took and held that —— trench last week, north of ——. Our Company led, as you probably know, and though I says it as shouldn't, since I had the honour of being in command, the work they did was absolutely top hole—they excelled themselves, and I want to tell you why.

"We got our orders the afternoon before—about five, and at half-past six the C.O. paid us a visit and gave the Company a little talk. We were back in ——, you know, luxuriating in the old Boche trenches and dug-outs, which, with a little repairing and scooping out, have made a first-rate rest place. Well, I wish I'd got a shorthand report of what the good old skipper said—By gad, you know, it is marvellous the way he's stood the strain of the last month, at his age. Positively seems to thrive on it. Brave! There isn't a boy in the Battalion more absolutely indifferent to crumping than he is. Where was I? Anyhow, it was all about you, and between ourselves

I don't mind confessing to you there was a certain amount of sniffling before he was through with it. You remember those Saturday morning talks of yours to the Company in 'A' and 'B's' dining-room at home. We knew the C.O. looked in once or twice, but I don't think anyone knew just how much notice he used to take. I tell you there wasn't much went on in the camp that he missed.

"Well, he reminded the men of some of the things you used to tell 'em, and talked about how we'd lived up to it so far in France, and the responsibility that rested on us as first Company in a Regular Battalion of a great Regiment and all that, you know. Paid what I think they call a graceful tribute to the Service Battalions, too, he did. And then he wound up with a little about the job we were in for in the morning; what an honour it was for the Battalion to have been selected by the Brigadier, and what a double honour for 'A' Company to lead it, and so on. We were all rather worked up, you know. And then it was he rung it in about you to top off with; said how grieved you were to be out of it; how he'd written to tell you what 'A' was to do; how you'd be thinking about us in your bed there in London; how we wished you could be there to lead us, and how, by God, every man of us would go into that show to do you proud, you know, and more careful than if you really were watching us, and all that.

"I wish I could give you his words, by Jove I do. But it was fine; I can tell you that. The C.O. himself was blowing his trumpet with the dirtiest old handkerchief you ever clapped eyes on; the C.S.M. nearly choked himself trying to stand fast at attention with a good chest on him; and as for little Sammy—there isn't a better platoon commander in the Battalion than little Sammy is to-day—he was fairly crumpled up. Had to edge round behind the C.O. to hide his blooming emotions, as they say. Oh, it was what the men call a great 'do' all right, and seriously I'm awfully glad the old man did it.

"You've heard how we got on, of course. 'C' and 'D' suffered pretty heavily, I'm sorry to say—worse than we did. It was a complicated job. We had to rush the trench first, followed

NEWS FOR HOME O.C. COMPANY 149

by ' B '; then we had to rush the support trench and keep Boche as busy as we could there, while ' C ' and ' D ' cleaned up and consolidated the front line, which was to be permanently held. As it turned out, the Boches had considerable difficulty with their men. The beggars simply wouldn't turn out of the dugouts to face us. We found barely five-and twenty men in the front line, and those, of course, we absolutely smothered; took 'em in our stride, you know. I got one myself with my trench dagger, and the C.S.M. who was next to me killed three to my certain knowledge. I saw it.

"Well, in next to no time we were in their support line with very few casualties. (Sorry to say Sergeant —— was killed between the two trenches.) And there we had some show, I can tell you. Curious there should be so much difference between the spirit of the Boches in two trenches next to one another. In that second trench, I won't say they fought like soldiers and men, because honestly they didn't; but they fought like mad beasts. At least they fought hard, I'll say that for 'em. In the front line they funked it at first. But their N.C.O.'s got 'em up to some purpose, while 'C' and 'D' were cleaning up there and making good.

"But in our line they fought hard from the word go, and they fought like beasts. I lost my own temper pretty badly, and as you know I'm pretty easy going. Two of the swines found little Jimmy (you remember Jimmy in

NEWS FOR HOME O.C. COMPANY 151

No. 3) lying beside a traverse, wounded. They both leaped at him, seeing that he couldn't possibly defend himself, and started slashing him through and through with their bayonets—poor little chap. That let me out, and I tackled those two for you and myself together. I was much too late to save Jimmy; but those two Boches will never stir again.

" There was a lot of that sort of thing. As I say, they fought like mad beasts, not like soldiers. I can't help thinking they must have had some drugs or something given 'em before we attacked—I never saw such brutes. And I never saw our chaps in finer form. Gad! it would have done your heart good to see them. Your name was shouted half a dozen times. We cleaned out every living thing before we finished, and I really think we could have held that second line till morning; but I had my orders, and, anyhow, an orderly came along from the C.O. with a message that I was to retire to the front line and help 'C' and 'D' consolidate. There were still a few Boches coming up from deep dug-outs there, and I think 'C' and 'D' were rather glad of our help in the clearing up.

"The Boche countered five separate times, and each time we let him get pretty close and fairly mowed him down with Lewis's and bombs. No exaggeration—they were thick on the ground, like mown corn. We were specially glad of the way the show went, partly because the Boches had been such unutterable beasts there, and partly, too, because I'm certain every

NEWS FOR HOME O.C. COMPANY 153

man of ours strained an extra pound or two on the strength of what the C.O. had said about you overnight."

CHAPTER XIII

" STICKFAST " AND HIS OFFICER

A R.A.M.C. OFFICER on board one of the hospital ships at Southampton put me into touch with three of its passengers whom one would have been sorry to miss.

They lay in different parts of the ship. All were weakened by loss of blood and considerably knocked about; all were smoking cigarettes when I saw them, and neither could have been in higher spirits if they had been twelve-year-old schoolboys arriving home for the summer holidays.

The senior is one of the oldest privates in our New Armies; the junior is one of our youngest officers, for he celebrated his nineteenth birthday in a front line trench in France last June. His friends may fairly be proud of him, for though only in his twentieth year he has already proved himself a brave officer and a gallant gentleman. When the war began this officer had just left school—within the week of the declaration—and a few weeks later he was to have entered a merchant's counting-house in a busy northern city. As things are, his experiences have been quite other than clerical. For nine months he has been a platoon commander in the fighting line in France. He was wounded once before, early this year, but so slightly that a week out of the line in a field ambulance put him right again. Now he will enjoy a somewhat longer rest, but he reckons on being back in the line in a month. "Don't want to miss *all* the fun, you know"—and a surgeon told me he will probably have his wish.

He told some stirring things about the conduct of his men in the fighting round Longueval. But what one wants to tell here is something about his own conduct, as one learned of it from the man most intimately concerned, and an eye-witness who was that man's section commander.

It was guesswork to call Pte. ——, of the —th ——s, one of the oldest men in the New Armies, for one did not ask his age; but his hair, or what little one could see of it under his bandages, is white, and his week-old beard and grizzled moustache and appearance generally are those of a man well past middle age. I'll wager he committed a gallant perjury when he enlisted, and that he will get a decoration for it in heaven!

"Well, it wasn't not what you'd call a regler attack, sir, it was more of a raid, like, that our Company was in that night—up to the left o' Longyvally it were. We was on the right, bein' in No. 3 platoon, sir, that's Mr. ——'s platoon, you know, sir. We wasn't to *take* their line, you understand, sir, but jus' to stir the Boches up a bit, as ye might say, an' find out what they was a doin' of an' put a stop to it; which I think we did put a stopper on it all right, sir, so far's them perticler Boches is concerned.

"Our a'tillery gave 'em taffy afore we started, sir, toppin' off wi' five minutes' hurricane fire, when you couldn't hardly hear yourself shout. An' then over we went, sir, my Mr. —— a-leadin', an' a proper young gen'elman he is, too, sir; as fine a officer as we've got, I reckon, for he never fails his men, he don't, he never forgets 'em, an' the best of everything that's going he gets for 'em; an' I don't see how a officer can do more'n that, whoever he be.

"I got a bullet through me left arm while we was crossin', an' that made me a bit awkward like wi' me baynit. But I got me Boche all right, sir, when we got to the trench—I did that, an' I stuck him twicet I did, for I wanted to be sure of him. An' jus' when I was drawin' me baynit back the second time an' wonderin' if I'd have any more luck, a big Boche sergeant come at me—I saw the stripes of him, sir, an' afore I could get me baynit back for a thrust he caught me over the head with the spiked club he carried. I saw the club, aye, an' saw it comin' for me head. Somehow I knew I couldn't stop it—couldn't get the baynit that high up quick enough, ye see. So I thought, ' Let be, then, we'll go together.' An' so I let drive wi' me baynit for his stomach. An' that's all I knew about it."

At this point one had to turn to the next cot but two, where the grizzled warrior's section commander lay with a broken ankle—a fair, red-haired, blue-eyed giant, of about three or four and twenty. Before he would tell me anything else, the section commander had to put one hand to his mouth whilst I bent down low towards him, by order, to receive in my ear in a hoarse whisper the following piece of information:

"You might think him queer, but a gamer old blighter never wore out shoe-leather—if you can foller me, sir."

The jerks of the section commander's head, his ponderous winks, violently twisted mouth, and gesticulating right thumb were upon the whole sufficient—to the entire ward, one would have thought—to indicate that he referred to my grizzled friend. A transparent person, the section commander—Heaven send him sound ankles and good luck wherever he may go! The elaborately set forth unconsciousness of his look across at the grizzled one, after his hoarse whisper to me, was a thing beautiful to see.

"As I was sayin', sir," he began, well

knowing he had said nothing of the sort as yet, " we made what you might call a nice clean job o' that bit o' trench, an' the dug-outs—remarkable clean job of the dug-outs, sir—with Mills 'and grenades an' plenty of 'em. An' after the 'and grenades, three men with the baynit in each, sir, so's to leave all tidy. Great one for tidyin' up, sir, is our officer. An' then he blew his whistle three times, sir, did Mr. ——. That was the signal to retire, an' we all climbed out beside him, just as he'd told us: hand an' knees outside. Mr. —— come out last, an' when we'd gone it might be ten paces, sir,

" ' Hullo ! ' says Mr. ——, ' where's old Stickfast ? ' he says, by which he meant to refer, sir, to his Nibs here, not meanin' any harm to the old boy, sir, not at all, but we call him 'Stickfast' because he never was known to fall out, or go sick, or give up. Nex' thing I knew, Mr. —— was runnin' as you might say hell for leather—if you can foller me, sir—for that Boche trench, yellin' 'Stickfast!' loud enough to startle the Kayser. But jus' before he started he'd said, 'You get on back to our lines, lads. Take 'em back, Sergeant,' he said to Sergeant ——

" 'Orders,' says the sergeant, sorter grumpy like. You could see he didn't like it, but off he goes with the platoon. Well, I stooped down to do up me bootlace, ye see, sir, an' I grabbed two men o' my section, an' told 'em—told 'em to do up theirs, ye see, sir. An' when we got back into the trench we was only a yard or two behind Mr. ——. 'Hullo, Corporal,' says he, friendly-like, like that, sir, 'what the hell are *you* doin' here?' he says; jus' like that. So, of course, I told him the sergeant sent us back to lend him a hand, and just then old Stickfast there did a bit of a groan, and a bunch o' Boches come round the edge of the traverse, feelin' their way with baynits well out, thinkin' we'd all gone.

"Then Mr. —— he lets out a yell you could hear a mile off. 'Let 'em have it, boys! Bomb 'em out! Give 'em hell! All the lot of ye!' says he, just as if he'd got a company behind him. I had one bomb left, be chance, an' gave it 'em over the traverse perlitely as I could, an' Mister Boches bolted like rabbits—couldn't see their tails for smoke. Old Stickfast wouldn't let go his rifle, so we had to yank it out of the big Boche he had skewered in the belly, an' then we lugged him out of the trench. Mr. —— has got the Boche's knobkerry—a beauty with spikes an inch long on it. Goin' back with Stickfast I got a bullet through me ankle, an' Mr. ——, he got another in the shoulder, an' Stickfast, 'e got one in his lef' hand. But otherwise we was all serene, an' I got in on me hands an' knees, with two Boche helmets. So we didn't do so bad. But we reckon Mr. —— would ha' gone back after Stickfast by himself if he'd had to walk to Berlin for the old man."

The Temporary officer is apt to be quite permanently a man, and the men he leads will follow his like while breath is in them.

CHAPTER XIV

A COOL CANADIAN

THEIR rollicking high spirits is certainly the thing that impresses one first and most about our wounded officers and men as they arrive. But there are other impressions. One notes a striking prevalence of true modesty. And upon investigation one often finds a deal of shrewd, direct thoughtfulness.

The second-in-command of a battalion which has been doing some hard and bloody fighting on the immediate flank of our Allies, down Guillemont way, was among the cot cases one talked with.

He had been rather badly knocked about by a German bomb at close quarters, but he allowed me to light a cigarette for him, and obviously enjoyed smoking it while we chatted.

"Efficiency, organisation, thoroughness—jolly good things in their place, you know," he said. "The Germans have them splendidly developed, and in the past perhaps we've been a bit lacking in this direction. But my own impression is that the folk who talk about the Huns having gone mad—being the mad dogs of Europe—they're not really exaggerating so much as you might suppose. I believe a tremendous number of Boches are to all intents and purposes mad. Tell you why.

"Their worship of efficiency and

A COOL CANADIAN

thoroughness—machine organisation—has carried 'em so far that they have entirely lost all sense of humour. Now, when a man really loses all vestige of the sense of humour, I tell you he's too nearly mad to be good company. It really is so. Complete absence of the sense of humour is in effect madness, or leads to it, anyhow. And that's what's the matter with the Boche to-day.

" When the Hun was practically having things his own way a year ago, you know, the news he gave the world was quite intelligible, and a good deal of it was to be relied on. He lies like the devil now in all his news. Well, that's all right; one can easily see why. But if you read his lies carefully—I've been reading 'em all the way between Amiens and here—you'll find they're the lies of a madman; they are quite mad lies.

"He says our offensive has been smashed; that we have given it up, having accomplished nothing at all; that we have failed to injure him in the least, have gained nothing, and are so appalled by the terrible casualties he has inflicted on us that we have finally given up in despair. Well, really, you know! Well, I ask you, do we look like it? Perhaps you'll say you can't judge. Well, you ask any man you like who comes from the front. I don't care how hard he's hit: he can't help knowing the preposterous absurdity of that sort of guff. Everybody on our side knows we hold the initiative and dictate every move. On the west front every move must be costly because it's all over ground fortified and prepared for a couple of years—an unending chain of fortresses really. But—we keep going forward, we never go back, and every hour, day and night, we are inflicting more casualties than we suffer.

"Thank goodness, at our worst, we never showed much sign of losing our sense of humour. I've been studying the Boche in the field for over a year, and I'm convinced he's lost his entirely, and that this is a worse loss than anything in ground or munitions. Indeed, I think it's fatal. His monstrous war machine is still immensely strong, and will go on working and destroying for a long time yet. But his individual fighters—they are either drug-and-machine driven maniacs, foaming and fighting as mad dogs fight, or in other places they are broken and despairing wretches who, in the absence of blows and pricks from their herdsmen, beg for mercy and capture. They've no sane medium left. Our chaps are all sane medium—cheery, game fighters with an active sense of humour which would redeem the worst sort of shambles. To the last gasp our chaps remain human, so do the French. The Allies will win if only because of that. They remain human—men and good fellows—no matter how much horror the mad dogs put up. 'Mad dogs' is not too strong, believe me. I've seem 'em spitting and biting. I know—by God I do!"

A Canadian captain with his left arm slung and a German officer's helmet in his haversack said:

"Oh, I'm a fraud—oughtn't to be here

A COOL CANADIAN 171

at all. There's nothing the matter with me but a bullet through my arm. And, anyhow, logically, I suppose I ought to be dead or a prisoner with the Huns. We took a trench north-west of ——, you know, and our chaps hurried on to the second line without orders. No doubt they thought they'd cleared the front line. I tried hard to get out after them, but it was an awkward place with a high, shaling bit of parados, and you'd hardly believe how important your left arm is till you try a job like that without it—my elbow was broken, you see.

" My orderly was with me. He'd got pipped through the shoulder outside the trench. While I squatted there I heard a scuffling underground just round the other side of the traverse I was leaning on. Took a look round the other side and found a Boche officer—the first I'd seen—just appearing at the mouth of a dug-out, feeling his way out. I could see the spikes of helmets behind him. So there it was. My revolver was empty. My orderly had lost his rifle away outside the trench. Awkward, wasn't it?

"Well, of course, I pointed my revolver at the Boche officer. One does that instinctively, I suppose. And to my surprise he said in English, 'Don't shoot!' I said I'd shoot the lot of 'em if one of 'em moved. 'You sit perfectly still. Sit right down where you are, Mister Boche, and I'll take you to England, but if you move you'll get six Service bullets, and my men will come along and bury you in your dug-out.'

"'Don't shoot,' he said in English."

"They sat down like lambs. I managed to whisper to my orderly, round the edge of the traverse, to get forward somehow and bring some men, and first of all to find me a rifle and bayonet, or a bomb, or a toothpick, or some blessed thing better than an empty revolver. 'Now do be careful, Mister Boche,' I said to the officer. 'I'm a conscientious objector when I'm at home, and I hate killing like the devil.' (I don't know for the life of me what made me tell him that.) 'But I shall be bound to give you six bullets if you budge one inch, and they're clumsy brutes, these Service bullets, they make a devil of a hole at close quarters, worse than two or three rifle bullets.'

"'We're not moving,' said the Boche. He seemed a bit sulky, I thought. So we sat and waited. My orderly had gone and nothing seemed to happen. I felt for my pipe with my left hand, but it was no go That arm was out of business. ' Got anything to smoke ? ' I said to the Boche, and as he moved I saw the risk, and told him pretty sharply to put down the rifle he carried. ' Over this way, please; gently now, along the ground—careful ! ' I told him. And so I got a first-rate weapon. Seems incredible I shouldn't have thought of that before, doesn't it ? That's why I say I ought logically to be dead.

" Well, after that we got on famously. He found a cigar, and gave it me; but I had to pretend I didn't like cigars, because with only one hand in working order I didn't dare to risk lighting it. But that Boche officer remained curiously sulky, I thought. I tried him on half a dozen subjects, and I know he could speak English as well as I could; but I couldn't get much out of him, except that he didn't like our artillery at all, and that he supposed we must be near the end of our ammunition. Oh, and he said that, now the Zepps had complete command of the air all over England, life must be pretty beastly for us there. I told him I thought they had managed to kill a few dogs and cats, a horse or two and so on; but that the only thing that worried our folk was that so few people had been able to see a Zepp, and they were all very curious to have a look at one. He didn't seem to like that.

"After a long time my orderly got back with three men and a corporal, and then I ordered the Boches to march out without their weapons. There were twenty-two of 'em altogether. I thought my empty revolver was rather a good joke, so I told the Boche officer about it then; but he only scowled and growled, and after that he was sulkier than ever, so we had no more talk."

CHAPTER XV

THE HOSPITAL MAIL-BAGS

A MEDICAL officer, whose duties take him to many of our military hospitals, has been good enough to obtain, and lend, extracts from a number of letters received by wounded officers and men from comrades in other hospitals.

All over the world the men and women of our race and our brave Allies are thinking, talking, and writing of the great offensive north of the Somme which began on July 1st. Histories are already in the making, no doubt. But one doubts if any of them will contain more direct human interest than could be found just now in the mail-bags of our military hospitals dotted over the face of Britain from Edinburgh to Torquay. Our wounded soldiers are enjoying an amount of leisure and rest which is, of course, entirely out of the reach of anyone serving at the front, and here, in our own country, a certain freedom in writing which can never exist in the neighbourhood of the enemy is permissible.

One finds in our hospitals and convalescent homes officers and men who were in close contact with the enemy three days ago, and others, again, who have not seen the trenches for three weeks, for three months, and even here and there those who left the front as long ago as the beginning of the present year. And

THE HOSPITAL MAIL-BAGS 179

among these patients, with all their differing stages of freshness from the fighting line, there are, of course, family ties in the military sense as well as the civilian sense. The military family is the division; its branches are the brigades; its households are the battalions. A., who counts the time he has been in Blighty by weeks or months, gives home news (in the civilian sense) to B., who as yet can only count his time in England by days, and B., fresh from his unit in France, gives home news in the military sense to A.

Thus a lieutenant in a Scottish hospital who arrived home wounded a few days after the present great offensive began, writing to a senior officer of his unit in a London hospital, newly arrived there from the neighbourhood of High Wood, after thanking his senior for news of the Battalion, says :

"Some of the things at home will puzzle you at first. Having time to read the newspapers right through makes a difference. I was awfully puzzled at first to find they still have tribunals and exemptions and things, and people grousing about the docking of holidays and week-ends and the terrible hardships of being taken away from their business for military service, and so on. But these things are only surface incidents, really, and don't mean much, though they make a good deal of noise. The country's perfectly sound at heart, I think, and I am told the munitions workers really are playing up like sports.

"One's got to remember, you know, that in spite of all that's happened our folk at home here have not *seen* war the way the people have in France. It makes all the difference. Also the whole idea of citizen military service is strange and new to them as touching themselves. They hear of married men of forty being called up for training, and they seem to think it's an unheard-of kind of heroism or martyrdom, or something. Dear souls! They're so extraordinarily sentimental.

"As you know, in our Battalion over sixty per cent. of the men were married and all enlisted before November, 1914. The proportion of over forty was very considerable, although the age limit then was—what was it?—something in the thirties, I know. They gave up their jobs and left their wives and families to lie about their age—bless 'em!—and to train with us without being told to by anyone, and nobody thought to call them heroes or martyrs, and I'm sure it never struck them that way, though they've been living in the trenches just on a year, and the new lot that get so much sympathy have been raking in the shekels at higher rates of pay than they ever had in their lives, during twenty months of war, and enjoying all home comforts.

"Queer, isn't it? And then to think of men a month or two over the age being keen to take advantage of the calendar *now!* And other chaps prating to the tribunals about their consciences and their businesses and things (mostly businesses, I think) *now*, after two years, and at the height of the Somme push! But the country as a whole is sound, and quite unalterably determined, and I think we can rely on it there'll be no slackening in the munitions output; and if I'm right there the Boche's number is up and nothing in the wide world can save him."

A sergeant on the South Coast, writing to his platoon commander in Manchester:

"It is three days now since I landed, sir, and I was very glad to have your letter this morning. You really must not worry about the platoon, sir. They would be very much upset if they knew you were worrying about them, because they would think you could not trust them, and, you know, sir, they are worth trusting. I left Lance-Sergeant —— in charge. He's come on wonderfully, and I asked Captain C—— if he would recommend him for full sergeant. He's worth it. The doctor here promises me that I can be out of hospital in a week or two, so I may get back before you. And, in any case, the platoon will do nothing to disgrace you, sir, you can rely on that. In the push up north of Pozières we had the right flank of the Company, and the Captain said we did splendidly. We had nine casualties, and I'm quite sure we got three times that number of Boches, besides eleven prisoners we took. After we'd got their front trench, Corporal S——— and three men of his section went out on their own—the moon was clouded then— and got a Boche machine gun from their second line and brought it back with three helmets. The corporal was slightly wounded, and the others not touched. The C.O. was told about it. They all want you back, sir, but the platoon's doing fine, and you must not worry about them. I think we've got the Boche fairly moving this time. He won't hold Thiépval much longer."

Private —— in Colchester to Private —— in London :

" I saw T—— D—— to-day, and he told me you were in London. How goes it, old sport ? I got a bit of shrap in my shoulder, but nothing to worry about. We had a great do outside Longyvally after you left. You remember that ridge on the right past where the reaper lay ? We had Master Boche on toast there. He came on at us in great blobs, like those stunts we did at Codford. We held our fire, and then let him have it at close range, four Lewis guns and our own rapid, hard as we could lick. My rifle burned my hand. You never saw anything like it, the way those Huns went down. Seemed a shame to take the money. And then, all of a sudden, ' Cease fire ! ' And the Captain yells out, ' At 'em, boys ! Finish the blighters ! ' he says. And over we went. It was a proper circus. We thought it was to be just a defence, and instead we took their blooming trench and fairly put the wind up the lot of them. You never saw the like. Half of 'em was baynited climbing over their own parados, fairly spiked to it, and the rest of 'em was prisoners; fair screaming for mercy they was. We held that trench for over an hour, and bombed right along their communications and blew in their dug-outs and two machine-gun emplacements. And while we were doing it ' B ' Company was cutting a sap out from our own front line, so's we had cover most of the way back. A great do."

From a subaltern in Glasgow to a subaltern in London:

"I've just heard I've got my second star; so you'll have to be a bit more respectful in future, my son. Three weeks in command of the Company, you know, with only one star—what a hero! Mind you, they did play up well. I'll never forget it. There wasn't a man in the Company but was trying to help me all the time, and as for the old C.S.M.—bless his Geordie heart!—I'd like to put up a statue to him. For three days before he was killed I don't believe he was ever off his feet. And, mind you, we were hard strafing most of the time. He did a bit of everything, the S.M., from bombing and machine gunning to burying Huns to get 'em out of our road. I got a couple of helmets, but I gave one to ——, because it was given me. The one I've kept I took on my own from the beggar who got his bayonet through my arm. I'll never go without a rifle and bayonet again. Had to tackle the beggar with my hands; but I finished him with my revolver, and after that I carried his rifle, you bet, and hung his pickle-tub, or whatever you call 'em, on my belt. There's lots of fight left in 'em, of course; but we've got 'em cold this time, I'm certain of it. The prisoners we take are jolly glad to get out of it. People say human nature's the same everywhere. Well, it isn't. You take it from me, these blooming Huns are not the same stuff as our men. Our chaps mostly want to go straight; they're all decent at heart. Boche wants to go crooked, and begad he does."

CHAPTER XVI

THE DIFFERENCE

As a listener only, I participated in a rather interesting meeting on the deck of a hospital ship just berthed at Southampton. Captain J——, who was invalided home from the western front in the spring of this year, was outward bound for the same sector of our front, and was given permission to board the hospital ship to meet Lieut. R——, a relative serving in the same unit, and homeward bound now, as the result of a wound received forty-eight hours earlier in the fighting north-west of Pozières.

THE DIFFERENCE

Salutations and first inquiries ended, the Captain said:

"Well, it seems I've missed the best of the fun. I strafed like blazes to get out in the beginning of July, but couldn't bring it off. And now, according to the newspapers, we're getting back to sort of pre-Push conditions."

"Who says so?"

"Oh, some correspondent or another."

"Well, I'll bet he hasn't been in the trenches much if he says that. There's nothing the same as it was, even in June, let alone when you were there."

"But what's the difference?"

"Oh, every mortal thing is different. It all *feels* different."

"But how?"

"Every way. For instance, there was

nothing but bare mud all round our trenches when you left, and long before the Push there was green stuff growing round everywhere; creepers and things straggling over the sides of the trenches; weeds sprouting everywhere. And that's been altered again since the Push; everything being ploughed in, as you might say, by the a'tillery."

"Yes, I suppose the heavy stuff has chewed it up a bit; but we saw plenty of that before I left. You remember how the Boche mortars and oil-cans smothered us the week before I left, below La Boiselle?"

"Oh, that! My dear chap, that was a rest cure. We used to notice a shell-hole then. What you notice now is a place where there's no shell-hole, and

THE DIFFERENCE

you don't often find it. And anyhow, of course, all the trenches you knew are away behind us now. One goes overland all round there. Even north of that's the same. Lancaster Avenue, Rivington, John o' Gaunt, Coniston, right along to Chorley, Chequer Bent, Lime Street, Liverpool Avenue, all those streets we worked in before you left—God, the water and the mud there was there—well, they'll never be used as trenches again, you know. All overland there now—stray bullets, of course; but just as safe as the villages we used to billet in."

"Yes, of course, you're further forward, but when one gets there I suppose it's much the same as the old places used to be?"

"Not the least bit. It's all totally

different. You see, we don't go into trenches now to hold a bit of line, as it used to be. We're on the move now, you see. Oh, no, we've done with that rotten old grind of everlastingly going back to the same old quagmires. Then, you know, we're on the high ground now. That makes an enormous difference. You can see the Promised Land, as Tommy says, see it all the time, and we're nibbling chunks out of it all the time. Oh, the chap who says it's as it was doesn't know what he's talking about. Nobody feels a bit the same, I can tell you. Why, our a'tillery's working now in places where the Boche a'tillery used to be, away ahead of their old front, you know—what used to be behind it.

"The main thing about the ground one

used to look out over was its emptiness. 'Member how desolate it used to look? Dead and empty like those Wells stories—before the earth had any people on it. Begad! it isn't empty now. We clear it up behind us, of course; the salvage chaps see to that; hundreds of tons of Boche rifles, equipment, and so on. And out in front you get the same mess, but different when the breeze is from that way, because of the number of dead Boches, you know. Lots of the ground we take is full of dead Boches before ever we get near it—dug-outs full, trenches full, shell-holes full—dead Boches everywhere; dead rats, too, by the thousand. And yet the Boches do their best to get in their own dead. They're pretty good at it. Like everything else they do—matter of policy, you know. The sight of so many dead is as discouraging to their troops as the stink of 'em is sickening to us.

"Oh, I can't tell you what the difference is, but you can take it from me there's nothing the same as it was, nothing at all. You've only got to look at our men to know the difference. They—well, they've become veterans, you know, real old warriors. Before, we went plodding along, pegging away, you know, because one had to do one's job; but now—now, we're winning the war, we're getting ahead—everybody knows it. I can't explain the thing, but you'll see what I mean directly you get out. We get held up here and there; we shall go on getting held up, of course. But there's no deadlock; you know we're getting on with it all the time,

THE DIFFERENCE

and the Boche is getting smashed up. Oh, it's different, all right."

Looked at on paper there is something curiously dumb and inarticulate about it all, but I could see the captain felt, as I did, that it certainly was "different." If the lieutenant could not explain very well, he was able to transmit his own conviction.

A letter reached me from a wounded officer who landed here recently, and was sent to a London hospital. He had been asked to let one know what impressed him most about the revolutionary change he passed through from the fighting line, north-east of Bazentin-le-Petit, to his present resting-place in one of the surgical wards of a military hospital in London.

" But the first thing is the bed, you know

—clean sheets and absolutely unlimited sleep. At first I had a dozen or more sleeps in the day as well as the solid night slabs of it. Even now I'm hogging it a bit in that respect. It is an absolutely glorious thing to feel the clean sheets all round you, and know you can sleep as much as ever you like. Then the baths. To wash as much as ever you like! I tell you you've got to go seven days and nights without ever taking your boots off or seeing soap or a towel, to know what this luxury means —it's priceless. And then the grub. It seems I'm a pretty fleshly sort of a chap, eh? Well, it's true, anyhow; I still find it a great joy to see a tray with a snowy cloth and shining things put down on my bed-table. It sounds piggish, but the eating of the nice clean food is a tremen-

THE DIFFERENCE 199

dous joy, just sitting there eating, with a book beside the tray too, and to feel you haven't got to hurry, or watch out, or listen, or arrange for any blessed thing at all. Sometimes I just sniff the sweet, clean air and enjoy that. I just lie, and let my eyes drift up and down the ward, hearing nothing, looking at nothing, enjoying everything—it's peace. I never knew what the word meant before. Nobody can who hasn't lived in the firing line. I've made up my mind what it is that sort of heals and recharges one more than anything else—it's being not responsible for anything or anybody. It's great."

CHAPTER XVII

WHAT EVERY M.O. KNOWS

THE public probably realise now a good deal more than they did before the present Allied offensive north of the Somme, as to the terribly far-reaching character of the destruction wrought by the kind of fighting that is waged on the western front. The wars of the past have been child's play by comparison with this kind of fighting.

One has grown accustomed to finding among the wounded a few men who have been struck down without ever being near the firing line. Transport men, quartermaster-sergeants, orderlies in villages behind the lines, and all sorts of people whose work keeps them well in rear of the fighting lines, have seen their share of death and destruction in this war. Even before the present offensive, and in parts of the line which were called "quiet," death came flying through the air from time to time, to scatter devastation in all kinds of unexpected places.

During the last few months our artillery has been making life extraordinarily difficult for the enemy, even in places situated two and three hours' march behind his fighting lines. In this work, one gathers from all new arrivals from the front, our gunners have established a very marked superiority over the Boche. Wounded airmen have told one that for every shell which has exploded during the past month in villages and rest places behind our front, fifty of our shells have landed, with deadly effect, among the Hun's lines of communication.

The fact remains, however, that, even on our side, the risks of shot and shell are by no means confined, in this war, to the combatants. Many of our stretcher-bearers take almost as much risk as the average private of the line, and our medical officers often carry on their labours in circumstances of the most deadly exposure.

I was talking with a newly-landed R.A.M.C. officer, who had carried on his work of tending and dressing wounded men for several hours, after being badly mauled himself by shrapnel splinters.

WHAT EVERY M.O. KNOWS

His point of view was different, of course, from that of the fighting man, but not less interesting and valuable, one thought.

"In a war like this, you know," he said, "one comes across all sorts of bravery quite outside killing and being killed. Perhaps the public hardly realises yet what a lot there is in soldiers' lives, outside fighting. I sometimes think the actual fighting is among the least severe of the strains placed upon the soldier.

"The recent fighting has been on such an epic scale, such a huge and devastating business——what's the word I saw in the papers this morning? 'Grandiose.' Yes, that's it—that I suppose it's natural the stay-at-home public should be apt to forget the merely human aspect. But it's there just the same. Our chaps remain just as human as ever, in their rough kindliness one to another, and—don't forget—in the different ills and disabilities to which humans are subject.

"Fighting makes plenty of demands for two-o'clock-in-the-morning courage, of course; but so do other things in this life at the front, I assure you. And, whereas the public hears something about the fighting heroism, it knows very little about the other kinds. Oh, well, they are all fighting courage, of a kind, of course.

"What I mean is this: toothache, neuralgia, dyspepsia, colic, stomach cramps, sick headaches, sore throats, whitlows, and homely little things of that sort, are not washed out by terrific bombardments and epoch-making advances. Not a bit of it. The world's greatest philosophers have often admitted that neither their philosophy nor anyone else's was proof against a stomach ache or the torments of an exposed nerve in a hollow tooth. Regimental officers will tell you that it takes a pretty full man's share of pluck and endurance, even when one is very fit, to 'stick it' cheerfully in some of the phases of an offensive like this.

"Well, I'd like the public to bear in mind what is known to every medical officer in the Army, that in every single unit on the front there are officers and men who are 'sticking it,' hour after hour, and day after day, with never an interval of rest or comfort, or anything to ease them, when, if they were at home, no matter how urgent or important their business, they would be in bed, or at least receiving such ease and comfort, such relief from pain, as medical attention can provide in civil life.

"I'd like everyone who is doing his bit at home, every man and every woman, to remember this. These brave fellows of ours they won't 'go sick,' you know, during an offensive. It's as much as one can do to get some of them out of the fighting line even when they are quite badly wounded, and as for the wounds of sickness—sometimes infinitely more exhausting and trying to bear—well, they just set their teeth and say nothing about these.

"In the last week, I assure you, I have been quite glad to see coming my way with wounds (so that I could get them the rest and medical attention they needed), soldiers, from colonels to privates, who to my certain knowledge must have been suffering horribly for days, and in some cases for weeks, without the slightest kind of alleviation of any sort, whilst keeping a stiff upper lip, and carrying on with never a spoken word that wasn't cheery, in all the din and fury of the front line; men with acute internal troubles, racking neuralgia, or violently painful things like whitlows, living on biscuits and bully beef in shell-pounded, sun-baked chalk ditches, for a week or so on end, half blind for lack of sleep.

"The very last man I dressed had a slight wound in the left hand. 'You might fix this up as soon as you can, will you, Doc.,' he said cheerily, to explain why he did not want to wait his turn. 'I must get back to my platoon as quick as I can. We've got a little raid on this evening.' A moment later he was vomiting. Well, I won't bother you with detail, but his case was perfectly clear. In ordinary life he'd have been in bed, and probably operated on, weeks before. I knew beyond any possibility of doubt the sort of torment he must have been suffering for weeks and the exact reasons why he looked such a scarecrow. I fixed him. I was his senior in rank, and when he tried to get away I placed him under arrest; begad, I did. At the clearing station, later on, I found out from his Company Commander, who was wounded, that, though everyone could see he was pretty ill, this lieutenant had never said one word about his condition or allowed anyone else to talk about it. He had just gone on with his job, day and night. 'About the best officer I've got, too,' said his Company Commander. 'Couldn't eat, himself; but he never missed seeing the last handful of his platoon's rations properly dished out. Oh, he mothered 'em well.'

"To a medical man some of these cases are wonderful. We know precisely what they mean. It's the kind of heroism that doesn't win decorations; but it's the real article all right, I can assure you, and this New Army of ours is full of it. I'd like the people at home to understand something about it. It should make it easier for them to stick their bit without bothering too much about missed holidays and things."

This medical officer had nothing to say about the quiet heroism of many of his comrades of the R.A.M.C. One has to look elsewhere for appreciations of that very real bravery.

CHAPTER XVIII

THE SOUTH AFRICAN

AMONG all the laughing, smoking, chatting, cheery thousands of wounded men one has seen land in England from the front I have met one who was sad.

This was a South African Company Commander who landed with shrapnel wounds in hip and ankle. It required some perseverance on my part to obtain any information at all from Captain T——; but the striking difference between his mood and that of all those round him impressed me, and I am glad I did eventually fathom the reasons of it. Apart from their general human interest, they throw a notable light on the relations existing between the officers and other ranks in our South African units.

The sector of new line that Captain T——'s company held north-east of —— was most furiously counter-attacked by the Huns after an intense bombardment. The third and fourth and fifth waves of the attack were broken by the company's trench fire, which included Lewis guns handled to the best possible advantage.

But still the Boches came streaming on, and accordingly the company rose out of their shallow trench and rushed forward a bit to welcome the invader, having learned on more than one occasion during the preceding week just how little the Hun likes the steel.

In that advance Captain T—— was struck down. As he lay helpless on the ground he saw plainly that the enemy's charge was broken, and he ordered his company back to their trench to save casualties. He yelled to his men to get back, and he sent a young lance-corporal (who had only earned his stripe during that same week) to ram the order home. So the defenders began to stream back unevenly as the word reached them.

Just then Captain —— saw two things. He saw four straggling Boches approaching him where he lay, and he saw the young lance-corporal (whose rifle had been smashed earlier on) deliberately returning to him from the direction of the trench. The Boches had doubtless recognised his uniform, and were anxious to kill or capture a captain. The young lance-corporal was coming on slowly and steadily, like a man drawn irresistibly by some kind of fascination.

"Get back to the trench, man! Get back!" shouted the captain. One of the Boches dropped on his knee to fire. The lance-corporal came steadily on. "Go back," shouted the captain as sternly as he could. "D'you hear me, corporal? That's an order. Go back, or I'll put you under arrest. Damn you, go back!"

The kneeling Boche fired twice, and missed. The lance-corporal—no more than a boy in years—looked back and forward. He had his orders, and was a well-disciplined, good lad. It was as though the sharp order had placed weights about his feet. So he swayed.

Then he gave one look at his captain—
" you know the way your favourite dog
looks at you if you order him back home
when, perhaps, you've a gun under your
arm ? "—and, in defiance of the discipline
which made an order tug at his feet, the
boy strode on again towards his captain,
glancing from the Boches to his officer,
as though measuring his chances.

The captain managed to level his
revolver. " It was worth a bluff to try
and get the fellow back."

" By God, corporal, I'll put a bullet
through you if you don't go back ! "

And at that the lance-corporal broke
into a run—but towards the fallen officer,
not the trench. He fell, with a bullet
through his heart, within three paces of
his captain. Two Boches were on their

knees firing at him then. The other two were advancing, crouchingly, on the captain. The captain had not yet used a round from his revolver, so he turned that now on the advancing Boches. But at that moment a Lewis gun in our own trench, firing pretty high, opened on that bit of No Man's Land. The incident had been seen, evidently. The fire was too high to hurt anyone, really, for the gunners feared to hit their own officer. But the Boches did not understand that. Their own gunners are a good deal less particular. So they turned tail and ran hard for their own trenches; while the captain, having emptied his revolver at them, lost consciousness, and knew nothing more of the business till he found himself in our own trench dressing station.

And now Captain —— finds it sadly hard to forget the solemn, puzzled face of the young lance-corporal who so deliberately elected to give up his life for his officer.

But I told the captain he must be very proud of that young lance-corporal, not sad about him. There have been many such noble deaths among the men of the New Army, and the bulk of them are in no way recorded—by mortal scribes. In other days, where our fighting has been always on a much smaller, less intense scale, it was possible to record a larger proportion of the heroic deeds done. But as a R.A.M.C. officer with whom I talked of this particular incident, after the wounded captain's train had started on its northern journey, said :—

"I think it's up to us as a nation to take good care that none of these sacrifices is wasted. Three parts of them will have no other record; but, if the people choose, they can make the nation's future the best possible sort of record, and the best sort of tribute and acknowledgment, too. All the nation has to do is to carry on, right through, in the same spirit that these chaps gave up their lives."

CHAPTER XIX

" IT'S A GREAT DO "

HIGH spirits would seem to be the rule among all who land in Blighty from out hospital ships. At least, I have come upon only one exception to this rule. But, in my recollection, high-water mark was reached by a certain laughing crew of bandaged merry-makers, who arrived on a sunny Monday morning at the end of summer.

The word " merry-makers " seems extraordinarily out of place in this connection. But what would you? They were all laughing and talking nineteen to the dozen. True, all were bandaged; the clothes of most were torn and bloody; many were unable to move from their cots. But all were laughing and talking with boisterous jocularity, and smoking cigarettes, and generally comporting themselves like exceptionally cheery and high-spirited holiday-makers on a pleasure excursion.

Here in England we discuss and speculate upon the fluctuations of the world's greatest war upon all its various fronts. The British soldier, even when at his weakest, from loss of blood and a long journey in hot weather, exults in the sure and certain confidence of victory, of steady progress toward glorious and final success. He has only seen his own little bit, of course; but he is magnificently happy about what he has seen.

" There's nothing on earth can stop us now, so long as the munitions keep going at full pressure," said a young captain, who knows that he has to lose his right foot, and is less cast down about it than the average civilian is over the prospect of losing a worn-out tooth. I have heard almost the same words, continuously the same emphatic conviction, from many scores of wounded men.

There was one particular party of private soldiers, with a lance-corporal and a couple of corporals among them, which, as a specimen group of our magnificent New Army men and as an illustration of the inimitable spirit that animates them, will remain always in one's memory. They were gathered together in the shade of a projecting portion of a boat-deck; all "walking cases," mostly bandaged for more than one wound; all ragged and blood-stained as to their uniforms, bronzed and weather-worn as to their hands and faces, with the indescribable fighting-line look in their eyes; full of laughter and good cheer, and carrying among them a wheelbarrow-load of souvenirs in the shape of Boche helmets, clubs, daggers, and the like. One half the party, I should say, were from the neighbourhood of Pozières, and the rest from the extreme right of our line, where we join hands with our gallant Allies, round and about Guillemont. Some of these last were no more than twenty-four hours from the actual firing line. All were glad to talk.

"It's a great do, sure enough; an' if Fritz has to put in another winter in the trenches he'll be a mighty sick man before it's over. I don't see how he's goin' to stick it."

"Come to that, how does he stick it now? 'Tain't because he likes it. What else can he do? You saw the machine gun chains. He's driven to his job like a beast, is the Boche."

"That's so. I'd be sorry for the beggar if he didn't play so many dirty tricks."

"Not me, mate. I'll never be sorry for the Boche. Seen too much of the blighter. If you'd seen the way he killed my officer, you wouldn't waste no bloomin' sorrow on him. Them as I've seen is as full o' dirty tricks as a cartload o' monkeys, or else they're foamin' at the mouth like mad dogs. A Boche is no good till he's dead, I say. We've bin too soft with 'em."

"What was it about your officer, then, Micky?"

"Mr. ——, as fine a lad he was as ever ye saw on p'rade, an' he knew how to take care of his platoon, too, I can tell ye. We was in their front line then, clearin' the trench. We'd took a whole lot o' the beggars prisoners, an' Mr. ——, he'd never let ye lay a finger on a Boche if the fellow made a sign o' puttin' up his hands, although he'd seen something o' their dirty tricks, too. 'No, by God!' he said, 'not in my platoon, Micky. It's a point of honour, Micky,' he says. Much they care for honour, the cruel beasts they are. We come to a dug-out that had the entrance to it half blown in, an' I was all for bombin' it first, and askin' questions after. But my officer, he wouldn't have it. He kep' in front, with me an' the rest o' No. 1 section behind him. 'Wo ist da?' he sings out down the dug-out, in their own lingo, you see. And one of the sausage-eaters he calls out, all so meek an' perlite, in English, you know: 'Only me, sir,' he says. 'Well, come on out, an' nobody'll hurt ye,' says Mr. ——. 'Cannot move, sir; very bad wound, sir,' says the Boche—damn him!

"Well, I wanted to go and see to the blighter, but Mr. —— saw the bomb in me hand, and didn't altogether trust me, maybe. 'Wait a minute, Micky,' says he; an' down he goes. Nex' minute I heard a groan, an'—'They've stuck me, Micky,' very faint like, from Mr. ——

"'Here, my God, boys!' I says to the

section, 'the —— swine has killed Mr. ——' Well, we just made one rush for that dug-out. One of 'em stuck me with his baynit, here, ye see, at the end of the passage. He'll do no more stickin'. I smashed his head with me butt. An' I got one other with me baynit. An' I could hear others runnin' like rabbits in the passages. I got one of ours to look after Mr. ——, though I could see he was done, and I sent the others back to the trench quick to see if they could catch any of the Boches getting out another way. Then one other chap an' me, we followed on where we heard 'em runnin', an' I don't mind tellin' you, what with seein' poor young Mr. —— an' the sting o' that Boche baynit in me side, I was seein' pretty red.

"There was two of the devils I'd got in the dug-out, an' there were five more altogether, one a sergeant. There was two o' my chaps waitin' for 'em when they got to the other entrance in the trench, an' my mate an' me we come along pretty close behind 'em. They squealed all right when they saw the point of Tim ——'s baynit in the sun just at the mouth of the dug-out, where they thought they was goin' to get clear. They turned an' come our way then, with Tim an' his mate behind 'em. An' then they met me an' my mate, an'—well, they won't meet nobody else this side o' hell. We fought like rats in that hole, an' poor Tim he was killed. I got chipped about a bit meself; but I was that wild about my officer, they hadn't got much of a chance, the dirty hounds!"

"Aye, 't'were a pity they got Tim an' the officer; a pity that." (The speaker was a very big man with a rough-hewn granite-like face—a farm-worker, I would say—by no means sad or gloomy; but of a reflective turn. His hands were enormous, and another man told me he had done great execution with them at close quarters. I could well believe it. He ruminated now apparently with great satisfaction.)

"There's nothing very civilised about 'em, even when they've lived in England. If England's got any sense there won't be any more of 'em live here yet awhile."

"Tom's goin' to stand for Parliament when the war's over!"

"I could teach 'em a bit about Boches if I did."

"Well, see you raise the bacon ration for us, Tom."

"An' you'll mention that little matter of the strawberry jam, won't ye?"

CHAPTER XX

ON THE WAY TO LONDON

For the time I was leaving behind me the long, trimly kept landing-stage at Southampton, with its acres of clean garnished sheds in which the wounded lie in serried ranks quietly awaiting the different trains. I was travelling with some of them in one of the smoothly running hospital trains bound for London.

From engine to guard's van the interior of the long train was immaculate, spotless, a triumph of scientific organisation, of carefully thought out, most admirably and consistently administered system. The accommodation was simply the very best, neither more nor less, that modern ingenuity can provide for the easy transport of the sick and wounded. For the General officer and for the private it was all precisely alike; not by reason of haste or emergency or accident, but because nothing better can be designed, and the authorities hold that the best cannot be too good for the soldier of whatever rank who is struck down in the performance of his duty; in the war which for us means the defence of civilisation against the onslaught of the modern Hun—the mad dog of Europe.

The train slowed down to a momentary stop, half in and half out of the station, at historic Winchester. A fast train from town had just previously passed through, bringing with it early editions of the evening papers. Our pause was hardly appreciable; perhaps we did not quite come to a standstill. But one enterprising orderly managed to obtain a single copy of an evening paper through a window near the guard's van. At that time I was at the far end of the train, near its engine, talking to some wounded men of a north country regiment.

In a matter of perhaps two minutes, it actually was before the train had regained its full speed, the news in that evening paper reached us there in the fore part of the train. I am not quite sure how it came. I started then on a walk through the train to its rear end. It is a pleasant privilege to carry cheery news to these devoted lovers of good cheer—the wounded. But it was I who was given the news; from every cot and with tumultuous enthusiasm among the sitting cases. No more than two minutes had elapsed since we glided through Winchester. But:

" Rumania's come in."

" Oh, yes; it's official."

" What about the Balkan-Zug and the highway to Baghdad now ? "

" Pretty good day for Serbia, this ! "

" Didn't some fellow say it would shorten the war by six months ? "

" The blackboard writers in the trenches will be busy to-night."

" News for Fritz, all right, to-day."

" This ought to show 'em the Allies don't mean to stop at any half measures. The Boche fighting machine has got to be smashed right up. They ought to see it coming, now."

"Well, I'm glad," said an elderly Colonel, with his right arm slung. And the cool, quiet satisfaction of his tone, so suggestive of a man's unalterable determination, was curiously impressive. "People have thought 'em slow, but I suspect they had excellent reasons for biding their time. You may be pretty sure they knew the best time. It's a sort of underlining of the letters of fire on the wall. Yes, I'm glad. I fancy the Boche will be able to read this."

I was unable to find a single man who had not had the news. One heard quietly cheery murmurs of "Good!" "First-rate!" and the like, even from the sort of "cases" one does not speak to, because they lie so still, or because, perhaps, a glance at labels or bandages has previously told one that their condition is serious.

"It's true, is it, about Rumania, sir?" said one muffled voice. And I recognised a corporal for whom, with some difficulty, I had arranged the smoking of a cigarette on the landing-stage. His bandages were a very complete disguise, and I had learned, what I think he had known for a day or two, that he would never see again. I was told this corporal had thrown a number of bombs, after the explosion which had robbed him for ever of his sight, and wounded him in half a dozen places. Inscrutable, incomparable courage, of the spirit that no devilishly inspired Boche device can ever quell! The very voice of this man was eloquent of modest but quite unquenchable good cheer. Being English, we cannot embrace such men; but to the end of our days we can pay them the homage of real respect. We can see to it, in strictly practical ways, that we never become wholly unworthy of their splendid sacrifices.

"Yes, Corporal; it's true." And then some sudden stir in one made one add: "And coming on top of what you did, there below Thiépval, Corporal, it's pretty good, isn't it?"

What they did there below Thiépval! He was only one of that heroic band; all humble, all modest, all invincible; merely invincible. I have talked with a number of them.

The truly great, the epic episodes of this vast war, are so numerous, so almost continuous, that the world cannot hope to know very much about nine-tenths of them. But, known or unknown, nothing truly great can ever really be wasted. It can never be as if it had not been. Never. The measure of these episodes cannot be taken. The limit of their results cannot possibly be set. Each is one impulse in the rhythmic symphony of pressure which is presently to rid the modern world of the most deadly peril civilisation has faced in our time or any other time. If there are left in Berlin sanely understanding students of the cataclysm, a knell must be rung in their hearts by all such episodes as that in which this simple English corporal (with no thought or desire in life but just, very simply, to do his duty), smitten to his knees and blinded by the explosion of a German shell, continued fighting, with the weapon he had been taught to use, till carried away, because he happened to be one of those who had been " detailed," as the phrase goes, to present a forthright English no! to the ferociously desperate assertion of the might of the vaunted Prussian Guard.

"No, we didn't let 'em through, sir; they couldn't get through us." That was as much as the corporal had to say about it, and it is not easy to induce any of his heroic comrades to say much more. That is their English way—God bless them! Yet from one here and there, from a gunner officer, from an intelligence officer of a unit not in the " show," and, for that matter, from the terse and pregnant lines of Sir Douglas Haig's own *communiqués*, we know that even this unparalleled war has yielded no more splendid instance of sheer endurance, of stark, unshakable bravery, than that wild week gave us below Thiépval, where German desperation saw its most concentrated efforts and the flower of its Army broken, wave after wave, against the cool, unalterable determination of the citizen soldiers of Britain's " contemptible little Army."

" The men were splendid ! "

www.ingramcontent.com/pod-product-compliance
Lightning Source LLC
Chambersburg PA
CBHW030407100426
42812CB00028B/2861/J